Accounting for AQA
A-level Part 2

Question Bank

Alison Aplin

osborne
BOOKS

© Alison Aplin, 2021

All rights reserved. No part of this publication may be reproduced, stored in a retrieval system, or transmitted in any form or by any means, electronic, mechanical, photo-copying, recording or otherwise, without the prior consent of the copyright owners, or in accordance with the provisions of the Copyright, Designs and Patents Act 1988, or under the terms of any licence permitting limited copying issued by The Copyright Licensing Agency, Saffron House, 6-10 Kirby Street, London EC1N 8TS.

Published by Osborne Books Limited

Tel   01905 748071

Email   books@osbornebooks.co.uk
Website   www.osbornebooks.co.uk

Cover design by Windrush Group (www.windrushgroup.co.uk)

Printed by CPI Group (UK) Limited, Croydon, CR0 4YY

British Library Cataloguing in Publication Data

A catalogue record for this book is available from the British Library

ISBN: 978-1-911198-92-5

Contents

		Questions	Answers
	Financial Accounting		
1	Financial statements and introduction to ethics	2	106
2	Incomplete records	7	109
3	Computer accounting	15	114
4	Partnership financial statements	18	116
5	Changes in partnerships	26	122
6	Accounting for limited companies	34	127
7	Statement of cash flows	46	135
8	Interpretation of accounting information	53	140
9	Accounting regulations and ethics	63	146
	Management Accounting		
10	Management accounting: the use of budgets	67	148
11	Absorption and activity based costing	79	158
12	Overheads and overhead absorption	85	162
13	Standard costing and variance analysis	92	167
14	Capital investment appraisal	98	171

Introduction

Accounting for AQA A-level Part 2 Question Bank has been written to provide supplementary examination practice material for students of AQA's A-level in Accounting.

The book is divided into two separate sections:

1 **Questions** appropriate for the AQA examinations, with gaps where students can write in the answers.

2 **Answers** to each of the questions, set out in the fully worked layout that should be used.

The book is also arranged in the chapter order of the main text book, **Accounting for AQA A-level Part 2** (see the Contents on the previous page).

Alison Aplin

Use of accounting terminology

The AQA examinations in Accounting make full use of international terminology as set out in International Financial Reporting Standards (IFRSs). The following shows the international terminology, together with the terminology used previously.

International Terminology	Terminology used previously
Financial statements	
Appropriation account (partnership)	Profit and loss appropriation account
Cash and cash equivalents (limited companies)	Cash in hand, cash at bank/bank overdraft
Financial statements	Final accounts and balance sheets
Income statement	Trading and profit and loss account
Inventory	Stock
Irrecoverable debt	Bad debt
Loss for year	Net loss
Non-current assets	Fixed assets
Non-current liabilities	Long-term liabilities
Other payables	Expenses due; income received in advance
Other receivables	Expenses prepaid; income due
Profit for year	Net profit
Revenue (within an income statement)	Sales
Statement of financial position	Balance sheet
Trade payables	Trade creditors (creditors)
Trade receivables	Trade debtors (debtors)
Accounting ratios	
Expenses in relation to revenue %	Expenses in relation to sales %
Profit to revenue %	Net profit to sales %
Rate of inventory turnover	Rate of stock turnover
Trade payable days	Creditor payment period
Trade receivable days	Debtor collection period

Practice questions

Financial Accounting page 2
Management Accounting page 67

FINANCIAL ACCOUNTING

QUESTIONS

CHAPTER 1: FINANCIAL STATEMENTS AND INTRODUCTION TO ETHICS

1. From the statements below select whether they relate to financial accounting or management accounting:

Statements		Financial accounting	Management accounting
(a)	Reports are produced in a standard format, usually on an annual basis above transactions.		
(b)	The purpose of this type of accounting is to assist in decision-making, planning and control.		
(c)	Reports are produced to meet the needs of a business for the use of internal stakeholders.		
(d)	There is often a legal requirement to produce reports for this purpose.		

2. Select the ethical principle which means that information about a business should not be disclosed to a third party:

A	Professional behaviour	
B	Objectivity	
C	Confidentiality	
D	Integrity	
E	Professional competence and due care	

3. A cash payment of £47 for stationery has been posted in the accounts as £74.

Which of the following correctly describes the type of error and the corrections to be made?

	Type of error	Entries to correct the error	
		Dr	Cr
A	Original entry	Stationery £47 Cash £74	Cash £47 Stationery £74
B	Commission	Stationery £47 Cash £74	Cash £47 Stationery £74
C	Original entry	Stationery £74 Cash £47	Cash £74 Stationery £47
D	Commission	Stationery £74 Cash £47	Cash £74 Stationery £47

4. The accountant for Micha's Electricals Ltd has been preparing the financial statements for the year ended 31 March 20-8 and has discovered that an irrecoverable debt of £1,065 should have been written off.

Prior to making the above adjustment, the balances in the general ledger accounts at 31 March 20-8 were:

Trade receivables £11,325

Provisions for doubtful debts £608

The provisions for doubtful debts should be maintained at 5% of trade receivables.

After making the correct adjustments, the balance on the provisions for doubtful debts account will be:

A	£566	
B	£970	
C	£513	
D	£1,121	

5. Oliver Limited prepares its financial statements to 31 May each year. At 31 May 20-8 its trial balance was as follows:

	Dr £000	Cr £000
Administration expenses	485	
Issued share capital – ordinary shares		400
Trade and other receivables	610	
Cash and cash equivalents	207	
Share premium		100
Distribution expenses	79	
Plant and equipment at cost	2,160	
Depreciation on plant and equipment		757
Retained earnings at 1 June 20-7		577
Purchases	2,438	
Inventory at 1 June 20-7	75	
Trade and other payables		215
Revenue		3,803
Dividends paid	236	
Finance costs	27	
Long-term bank loan		465
	6,317	6,317

Notes:

- Inventory at 31 May 20-8 cost £79,000.
- The tax charge based on the profits for the year is £162,000.
- Depreciation on plant and equipment has already been provided for in the list of balances above and allocated to administration expenses.

Required:

Prepare the income statement, statement of changes in equity and statement of financial position of Oliver Limited for the year ended 31 May 20-8 in the next pages:

CHAPTER 2: INCOMPLETE RECORDS

1. Beth has the following assets and liabilities at 1 March 20-7:

	£
Office equipment	4,000
Motor vehicles	15,000
Inventory	6,500
Trade receivables	3,600
Trade payables	1,400
Bank overdraft	8,200

   Calculate her opening capital at 1 March 20-7.

   ----

2. The following information was provided by Gary, a sole trader, for the year ended 30 September 20-8:

Capital at 1 October 20-7	£16,800
Capital at 30 September 20-8	£9,700
Profit for the year ended 30 September 20-8	£5,100

   What were Gary's drawings for the year ended 30 September 20-8?

A	£7,100	
B	£12,200	
C	£2,000	
D	£21,400	

3. Carys started a business on 1 January 20-8 and opened a new bank account on that date. A summary of her bank transactions for the year ended 31 December 20-8 were:

	£
Capital introduced	10,000
Payments to trade payables	26,510
Purchase of fixtures and fittings	14,000
Receipts from trade receivables	48,900
Drawings	7,800

Calculate her closing bank balance at 31 December 20-8.

---

4. Kayo, a sole trader, has not maintained proper books of account. The following information is available relating to trade payables for the year ended 30 November 20-8:

Trade payables at 1 December 20-7	£13,800
Trade payables at 30 November 20-8	£15,650
Payments to trade payables	£147,300
Purchases returns	£438
Discounts received	£1,685

The figure for purchases for the year ended 30 November 20-8 was:

A	£165,073	
B	£149,503	
C	£147,573	
D	£151,273	

5. The following information is available about wages paid for the year ended 31 August 20-8:

Amounts owed to employees at 1 September 20-7	£600
Amounts owed to employees at 31 August 20-8	£900
Expense in the income statement	£56,500

How much was paid out of the bank in respect of wages for the year ended 31 August 20-8?

A	£56,200	
B	£56,800	
C	£56,500	
D	£57,100	

6. A business has recently sold some equipment which cost £22,000 and had provision for depreciation at the time of sale of £14,000. The business made a profit on sale of £3,000.

The sale proceeds were:

A	£25,000	
B	£5,000	
C	£8,000	
D	£11,000	

7. Sales for the year are £500,000, the gross profit margin is 30%.

Calculate the cost of sales.

----

8. Revenue for the year is £200,000, the gross profit mark-up is 25%, opening inventory is £15,000 and closing inventory is £20,000.

   Purchases for the year are:

A	£160,000	
B	£150,000	
C	£165,000	
D	£155,000	

9. Jenny runs a florist and all takings are received in cash. Jenny banks the cash on a weekly basis after she has taken out any money required for cash payments.

   Jenny has supplied the following information for the year:

Cash in the till at the start of the year	£450
Cash in the till at the end of the year	£500
Takings	£54,600
Bankings	£46,200
Cash payments	£7,600

   During the year there was a break-in and some cash was stolen from the till.

   Calculate the amount of cash that was stolen.

10. Bernard owns a stationery business; he does not keep proper books of account.

The following information is available for the year ended 31 December 20-8:

	1 January 20-8 £	31 December 20-8 £
Inventory	14,250	18,910
Trade payables	5,600	7,850
Other payables – rent	0	1,000
Shop equipment at carrying value	56,800	41,700

A summary of the bank transactions for the year ended 31 December 20-8 are:

	Debit £	Credit £	Balance £
Balance at 1 January 20-8			8,968
Cash takings banked		336,236	345,204
Payments to trade payables	225,724		119,480
Drawings	42,000		77,480
Sale of equipment		680	78,160
Rent of shop	11,000		67,160
General expenses	15,326		51,834
Wages	44,000		7,834

- At 31 December 20-8 there are unpresented cheques to trade suppliers totalling £4,960 and amounts for cash takings not yet credited of £2,782.
- Bernard has taken some goods for his own use during the year, but he is unsure of the value of these goods.
- All purchases are made on credit and all sales are on a cash basis.
- The equipment sold during the year had a net book value of £1,200.
- Bernard's policy is to have a mark-up on all goods sold of 50%.

Required:

(a) Calculate the opening capital at 1 January 20-8 for Bernard.

(b) Prepare the trading section of the business's income statement for the year ended 31 December 20-8 to show the value of goods taken for own use by Bernard.

(c) Complete the income statement for the year ended 31 December 20-8 to show Bernard's profit or loss for the year.

(d) Prepare the statement of financial position for Bernard at 31 December 20-8.

CHAPTER 3: COMPUTER ACCOUNTING

1. From the statements below select whether each is an advantage or disadvantage of a computerised accounting system:

Statements		Advantage	Disadvantage
(a)	Knowledge of double-entry bookkeeping is not required.		
(b)	Users may not fully understand processes and errors are likely to occur.		
(c)	Most transactions only need to be input once, therefore time is saved.		
(d)	Reports can be produced automatically and tailored to the needs of a business.		

2. Bow Ltd is considering moving to a computerised accounting system. What costs could Bow Ltd incur?

3. Progress Ltd is planning to introduce an integrated computer accounting system. The operations director has been told about all the advantages by the software company but is anxious to know about the possible disadvantages.

You are to state two possible disadvantages of this proposal and explain how they could cause problems within the company.

Disadvantage 1

Disadvantage 2

4. Describe one benefit and one drawback of using spreadsheets to produce financial information.

Benefit of using spreadsheets

Drawback of using spreadsheets

CHAPTER 4: PARTNERSHIP FINANCIAL STATEMENTS

1. Select whether the following statements are true or false about the Partnership Act 1890:

Statements		True	False
(a)	Profits or losses are shared in the same proportion as the capital which has been contributed by each partner.		
(b)	No partner is entitled to any drawings.		
(c)	Partners may be entitled to a salary.		
(d)	Partners are not entitled to receive interest on their capital.		

2. Mike and Bryan are in partnership, sharing profits on an equal basis. Any drawings are charged interest at 5% per annum, Mike had drawings of £12,000 during the year and Bryan had none.

    Partnership profits for the year were £53,400; Mike and Bryan will each receive a share of the remaining profits of:

A	£26,700	
B	£27,000	
C	£26,400	
D	£32,700	

3. In the first year of a partnership, the following information is available about one of the partners, Margaret:

Drawings	£15,000
Salary	£16,000
Interest on drawings	£300
Interest on capital	£2,250
Share of profit	£19,000

What is the balance on Margaret's current account at the end of the year?

A	£21,950	
B	£22,550	
C	£36,950	
D	£18,050	

4. Alison, Bernadette and Coleen are in partnership and share profits on the following basis:

	Alison	Bernadette	Coleen
Salary	£10,000	£nil	£20,000
Share of profits	30%	50%	20%

They are also entitled to interest on their capital accounts of 3% per annum. The capital account balances at the start of the year were:

	Alison	Bernadette	Coleen
Capital	£10,000	£30,000	£10,000

The partnership profit for the year ended 31 March 20-8 was £66,500.

Prepare the partnership appropriation account for Alison, Bernadette and Coleen for the year ended 31 March 20-8, on the next page.

5. Eliza and Sam are in partnership called 'ES Hairdressers'.

The following information is available for the year ended 31 December 20-8:

	Eliza £	Sam £
Capital accounts at 1 January 20-8	40,000 Cr	30,000 Cr
Current accounts at 1 January 20-8	480 Dr	1,310 Cr
Drawings	12,000	28,640
Partnership salary	8,000	0
Interest on drawings	600	1,432
Interest on capital	2,400	1,800

The remaining profits are shared in the ratio of 60% to Eliza and 40% to Sam.

The partnership profit for the year ended 31 December 20-8 was £41,268.

Prepare the partners' capital and current accounts for the year ended 31 December 20-8:

6. Ayesha and Josh are in partnership running a bookshop called 'Obscure Fiction'. The following trial balance has been taken from their accounts for the year ended 31 March 20-8:

	Dr £	Cr £
Capital account: Ayesha		25,000
Capital account: Josh		25,000
Current account: Ayesha	450	
Current account: Josh		180
Drawings: Ayesha	6,845	
Drawings: Josh	13,050	
Purchases	36,750	
Revenue		79,800
Opening inventory	5,865	
Wages	7,380	
Rent and rates	8,300	
Sundry expenses	585	
Discounts received		524
Credit card charges	880	
Motor expenses	689	
Equipment at carrying value	24,800	
Trade payables		2,890
Bank	27,800	
	133,394	133,394

Notes at 31 March 20-8:

- Inventory was valued at £6,273.
- Wages owing were £56.
- Prepaid rent was £500.
- Depreciation is to be charged on the equipment at 25% per annum, using the reducing balance method.
- Josh is to receive a partnership salary of £6,000.
- Interest is to be allowed on partners' capital accounts at 5% per annum, there is no interest on partners' drawings.
- Remaining profits and losses are to be shared equally.

Required:

Prepare the income statement, partners' capital and current accounts and statement of financial position of Obscure Fiction for the year ended 31 March 20-8.

CHAPTER 5: CHANGES IN PARTNERSHIPS

1. From the statements below select the one which is correct about goodwill:

(a)	Goodwill is the net assets of a business, the assets less liabilities.	
(b)	Goodwill is the amount that is contributed into a business by the owners.	
(c)	Goodwill is the difference between the value of a business and the net value of its separate assets and liabilities.	
(d)	Goodwill is the total value of non-current assets owned by a business.	

2. Annie, Bertie and Clive are in partnership and Bertie decides to retire. The agreed valuation of goodwill is £50,000 and the profit sharing ratios are:

	Old profit sharing ratio	New profit sharing ratio
Annie	40%	60%
Bertie	40%	
Clive	20%	40%

The goodwill adjustments in Clive's capital account are:

A	Dr £30,000,	Cr £20,000	
B	Dr £NIL,	Cr £20,000	
C	Dr £10,000,	Cr £20,000	
D	Dr £20,000,	Cr £10,000	

3. Donald is retiring from a partnership, he has a balance on his capital account of £30,000 and is paid £50,000 from the partnership bank account on the date he retires. Donald's share of the goodwill created at the date of his retirement is £45,000. Any remaining balance on Donald's capital will be transferred to a loan account.

    How much will the partnership owe to Donald in the form of a loan?

A	£Nil
B	£25,000
C	£35,000
D	£75,000

4. Drita and Elizabeth are in partnership sharing profits 50:50, they each have a balance on their capital accounts of £30,000.

    Fred joins the partnership and introduces £50,000 into the bank. The new profit sharing ratio is:

    Drita   60%

    Elizabeth   20%

    Fred   20%

    Goodwill has an agreed valuation of £64,000 and non-current assets have been revalued, creating a surplus of £15,600. It has been agreed that a goodwill account is not to be maintained in the books of account.

    Prepare the partners' capital accounts, after the above transactions have taken place.

5. The following information is available about the 'IT for Novices' partnership for the year ended 31 December 20-8:

- The partners at the beginning of the year were Xaviar and Yan.
- Zain joined the partnership on 1 April 20-8.

Partners' annual salaries:	£
Xaviar	18,000
Yan	24,000
Zain	12,000

Partners' interest on capital (for a full year):	£
Xaviar	960
Yan	840
Zain	600

Profit share to 31 March 20-8:	%
Xaviar	70
Yan	30

Profit share from 1 April 20-8:	%
Xaviar	60
Yan	20
Zain	20

The profit for the year ended 31 December 20-8 was £120,000.

Prepare the partnership appropriation account for the year ended 31 December 20-8.

Partnership Appropriation Account for the year ended 31 December 20-8

Period 1: 1 January – 31 March 20-8 (3 months)

	£	£
Profit for the period (£120,000 × 3/12)		30,000
Less: Salaries		
Xaviar (18,000 × 3/12)	4,500	
Yan (24,000 × 3/12)	6,000	(10,500)
Less: Interest on capital		
Xaviar (960 × 3/12)	240	
Yan (840 × 3/12)	210	(450)
Profit available for sharing		19,050
Share of profit:		
Xaviar (70%)	13,335	
Yan (30%)	5,715	19,050

Period 2: 1 April – 31 December 20-8 (9 months)

	£	£
Profit for the period (£120,000 × 9/12)		90,000
Less: Salaries		
Xaviar (18,000 × 9/12)	13,500	
Yan (24,000 × 9/12)	18,000	
Zain (12,000 × 9/12)	9,000	(40,500)
Less: Interest on capital		
Xaviar (960 × 9/12)	720	
Yan (840 × 9/12)	630	
Zain (600 × 9/12)	450	(1,800)
Profit available for sharing		47,700
Share of profit:		
Xaviar (60%)	28,620	
Yan (20%)	9,540	
Zain (20%)	9,540	47,700

Summary of totals credited to partners' current accounts

	Xaviar £	Yan £	Zain £	Total £
Salary	18,000	24,000	9,000	51,000
Interest on capital	960	840	450	2,250
Share of profit (Q1)	13,335	5,715	–	19,050
Share of profit (Apr–Dec)	28,620	9,540	9,540	47,700
Total	**60,915**	**40,095**	**18,990**	**120,000**

6. Peggy and Nora are in partnership trading as 'Our Local Café' and Queenie joined the partnership on 1 January 20-8. The following trial balance has been taken from their accounts for the year ended 31 December 20-8:

	Dr £	Cr £
Capital introduced: Queenie		44,500
Capital account at 1 Jan 20-8: Peggy		15,000
Capital account at 1 Jan 20-8: Nora		15,000
Current account at 1 Jan 20-8: Peggy		580
Current account at 1 Jan 20-8: Nora		630
Drawings: Peggy	33,000	
Drawings: Nora	32,000	
Drawings: Queenie	17,000	
Purchases	151,438	
Revenue		266,700
Opening inventory	10,200	
Wages	29,200	
Office costs	10,196	
Sundry expenses	1,386	
Property	30,000	
Trade payables		15,560
Bank	43,550	
	357,970	357,970

Notes at 31 December 20-8:

- Inventory was valued at £15,300.

- Peggy took goods for her own use totalling £750.

- On 1 January 20-8 the property was revalued at £50,000 and goodwill was valued at £65,000, neither of these transactions have been reflected in the accounts. Goodwill is not to be maintained in the books of account.

- All profits were shared 50/50 between Peggy and Nora.

- The new profit sharing ratio is Peggy (40%), Nora (40%), Queenie (20%).

Required:

Prepare the income statement, partners' capital and current accounts and statement of financial position of 'Our Local Café' for the year ended 31 December 20-8.

CHAPTER 6: ACCOUNTING FOR LIMITED COMPANIES

1. International Accounting Standard (IAS) 1 states that a complete set of financial statements should include:

		True	False
(a)	Statement of changes in equity		
(b)	Statement of cash flows		
(c)	Auditors' report		
(d)	Income statement		
(e)	Appropriation account		
(f)	Statement of financial position		
(g)	Statement of affairs		
(h)	Accounting policies and explanatory notes		

2. From the definitions below, select the one that correctly describes the accruals accounting concept:

(a)	Financial statements should not include the personal expenses or income or, record personal assets and liabilities for any of the people involved in owning or running a company.	
(b)	Only transactions which can be measured in monetary terms can be included in the financial records or statements.	
(c)	Financial statements should take a conservative approach where there is any doubt in the reporting of profits or the valuation of assets.	
(d)	Financial statements are prepared on the basis that income and expenses occurring in the same accounting period are matched.	

3. Select whether the following statements are true or false about limited company accounts:

Statements	True	False
(a) A copy of the management accounts must be filed with Companies House.		
(b) Private limited companies must file statutory accounts with Companies House within six months of the end of their accounting period.		
(c) The accounts of all companies must be audited by external auditors, who are appointed by the shareholders and form an opinion on the company's financial statements.		
(d) The legal and regulatory framework sets out the rules which must be followed when preparing limited company accounts.		

4. Terry has just been appointed as a director of a limited company.

   (a) Briefly state the responsibilities of directors under the Companies Act 2006.

   (b) List the items that should be contained within the directors' report which is included in the published accounts of a company.

5. Suggest two external and two internal stakeholders of a limited company and state why they may be interested in the financial statements.

External stakeholders

Internal stakeholders

6. List and explain two benefits and two limitations of published accounts.

Benefits

Limitations

7. Q Ltd has the following information available about its share capital:

	£
Authorised capital – Ordinary shares of 25p each	250,000
Issued capital – Ordinary shares of 25p each	200,000

Q Ltd has offered all existing shareholders' a rights issue at 50p per share on the basis of one new share for every eight held.

Assuming that all shareholders take up the rights issue, Q Ltd will receive:

A	£25,000	
B	£50,000	
C	£62,500	
D	£31,250	

8. The equity section of the statement of financial position of Georgie Ltd at 1 January 20-8 is shown below:

	£
Ordinary shares of 10p each, fully paid	300,000
Share premium	50,000
Retained earnings	41,000
Total equity	391,000

On 1 April 20-8, a bonus issue was completed. The shares were issued on the basis of one new share for every five shares held.

During the year ended 31 December 20-8 land and building were revalued with an increase of £200,000, dividends paid were £240,000 and the profit for the year was £285,000.

At the end of the year a final dividend of £63,000 was proposed.

Prepare the statement of changes in equity of Georgie Ltd for the year ended 31 December 20-8.

9. The directors of Fitness plc have provided the following statement of financial position extracts:

	31 May 20-7 £000	31 May 20-8 £000
Non-current assets carrying amounts:		
Land and buildings	225	343
Plant and equipment	188	240
	413	583

Additional information:

- Land and buildings were revalued at £350,000 on 1 June 20-7, their original cost was £250,000.

- Land and buildings are depreciated using the straight-line method at 2% per annum.

- The cost of plant and equipment at 1 June 20-7 was £425,000.

- In the year to 31 May 20-8, plant and equipment which had originally cost £40,000 was sold. The depreciation charge on these non-current assets was £10,000.

- In the year to 31 May 20-8, plant and equipment was purchased at a cost of £162,000.

- Plant and equipment are depreciated using the reducing balance method at 25% per annum.

Complete the detailed note for the published accounts of Fitness plc for the year ended 31 May 20-8, which shows the movement in the carrying amounts of land and buildings and plant and equipment, using the template provided on the next page:

Fitness plc

Non-current assets note for the year ended 31 May 20-8

	Land and buildings	Plant and equipment	Total
	£000	£000	£000
Cost			
At 1 June 20-7			
Additions at cost			
Less Cost of disposals			
Revaluation			
At 31 May 20-8			
Depreciation			
At 1 June 20-7			
Charge for the year			
Less Eliminated on disposal			
Less Eliminated on revaluation			
At 31 May 20-8			
Carrying amount at 31 May 20-8			

10. Victor Ltd prepares its financial statements to 31 March each year. At 31 March 20-8 its trial balance was as follows:

	Dr £000	Cr £000
Administration expenses	131	
Ordinary shares of £1 each, fully paid		300
Trade and other receivables	194	
Bank overdraft		48
Share premium		150
Distribution expenses	122	
Finance costs	2	
Property cost	380	
Plant and equipment cost	750	
Depreciation on plant and equipment		485
Retained earnings at 1 April 20-7		107
Purchases	484	
Inventory at 1 April 20-7	57	
Trade and other payables		82
Revenue		1,084
Dividends paid	136	
	2,256	2,256

Further information:

- Inventory was valued at £65,000 on 31 March 20-8.
- Irrecoverable debts of £17,000 are to be written-off to administration expenses.
- The tax charge based on the profits for the year is £35,000.
- The property is to be revalued to £450,000.
- Depreciation of plant and equipment is to be provided for the year at 20% on a straight-line basis and is to be apportioned equally to administration expenses and distribution expenses.

Required:

Prepare the income statement, statement of changes in equity and statement of financial position of Victor Ltd for the year ended 31 March 20-8.

CHAPTER 7: STATEMENT OF CASH FLOWS

1. Which of the following statements correctly describes the types of inflows and outflows that are included in the financing section of a statement of cash flows:

(a)	The changes in cash and cash equivalents for the period.	
(b)	The main revenue producing activities and the payments of interest and tax.	
(c)	Receipts from the issue of new shares, payments to repay share capital, changes in non-current liabilities and the payment of dividends.	
(d)	The purchase and sale of non-current assets and other investments, and interest and dividends received.	

2. Pete Ltd has the following information relating to the year ended 30 November 20-8:

	£
Loss from operations	6,846
Depreciation	5,064
Loss on sale of non-current assets	782
Decrease in inventory	2,889
Increase in trade receivables	3,015
Increase in trade payables	2,930

The cash from operating activities included in the statement of cash flows is:

A	£15,496	
B	£(1,000)	
C	£(3,804)	
D	£1,804	

3. The following information has been extracted from the statement of financial position of Hood Ltd for the year ended 31 December 20-8:

	31 December 20-8 £	31 December 20-7 £
Current assets – Bank	9,084	–
Current liabilities – Bank overdraft	–	5,127
Non-current liabilities – Bank loan	55,685	52,134

The net increase/(decrease) in cash and cash equivalents included in the statement of cash flows for the year ended 31 December 20-8 is:

A	£(14,211)	
B	£(10,660)	
C	£10,660	
D	£14,211	

4. Trent Ltd has the following activities for the year ended 31 October 20-8:

	£
Proceeds from the sale of non-current assets	8,500
Receipts from the issue of share capital	102,000
Purchase of non-current assets	86,000
Repayment of non-current loans	5,000
Dividends paid	27,600
Dividends received	1,200

The figure for investing activities included in the statement of cash flows is:

A	£(76,300)	
B	£69,400	
C	£(6,900)	
D	£(103,900)	

5. Perry Ltd has the following information for the year ended 30 June 20-8:

	£
Proceeds from the sale of non-current assets	6,200
Receipts from the issue of share capital	10,250
Purchase of non-current assets	2,500
Increase in non-current loans	6,000
Dividends paid	15,000
Interest received	750

The figure for financing activities included in the statement of cash flows is:

A	£4,450	
B	£5,700	
C	£1,250	
D	£4,250	

6. Extracts from the statement of financial position of Daffodil Ltd regarding property, plant and equipment (PPE) for the year ended 31 March 20-8 are as follows:

	31 March 20-8	31 March 20-7
PPE – carrying amount	£63,107	£57,248

The income statement includes the following:

	31 March 20-8
PPE – depreciation	£7,283
Profit on sale of non-current assets	£250

During the year property, plant and equipment was disposed of with a carrying amount of £1,800.

Calculate the figures for proceeds from the sale of non-current assets and purchase of non-current assets to be included in the statement of cash flows for the year ended 31 March 20-8.

7. The statement of financial position of Ninety Ltd for the last two years are:

Statement of Financial Position as at 31 December 20-8

	20-8 £000	20-8 £000	20-7 £000	20-7 £000
Non-current assets				
Cost	8,570		7,825	
Depreciation to date	(1,569)	7,001	(1,321)	6,504
Current assets				
Inventory	118		129	
Trade receivables	333		301	
Cash and equivalents	64		107	
		515		537
TOTAL ASSETS		7,516		7,041
EQUITY				
Ordinary shares		1,700		1,500
Share premium		280		250
Retained earnings		4,162		4,275
TOTAL EQUITY		6,142		6,025
Non-current liabilities				
Loans		1,002		687
Current liabilities				
Trade payables	94		78	
Tax liability	278		251	
		372		329
		7,516		7,041

Further information:

- Additional non-current assets were purchased at a cost of £784,000.

- Non-current assets, which had been depreciated by £28,000 were sold for £14,000.

- There were no other disposals or purchases of non-current assets.
- Taxation paid totalled £353,000.
- Dividends paid totalled £1,386,000.
- The income statement for the year ended 31 December 20-8 included:

    depreciation charges £276,000

    finance costs £152,000

    taxation provision £380,000

Required:

Prepare the statement of cash flows for Ninety Ltd for the year ended 31 December 20-8.

CHAPTER 8: INTERPRETATION OF ACCOUNTING INFORMATION

Use the information below about Whitey plc to answer questions 1 to 5:

Current market price per share	£4.80
Profit for the year before interest and tax	£630,000
Profit for the year after tax	£450,000
Dividend on ordinary shares for the year	£360,000
Number of issued ordinary shares of £1 each	300,000
Interest payable for the year	£20,000

1. The dividend yield of Whitey plc is:

A	25.00%	
B	31.25%	
C	43.75%	
D	80.00%	

2. The earnings per share of Whitey plc is:

A	£1.20	
B	£1.50	
C	£2.10	
D	£3.80	

3. The dividend cover of Whitey plc is:

A	1.25 times	
B	1.50 times	
C	1.75 times	
D	4.00 times	

4. The price earnings of Whitey plc is:

A	1.25	
B	3.20	
C	4.00	
D	4.80	

5. The interest cover of Whitey plc is:

A	1.25 times	
B	1.75 times	
C	22.50 times	
D	31.50 times	

6. Which of the following statements correctly defines liquidity?

(a)	The financial stability of a business on a long-term basis.	
(b)	A measure of the surplus of income over expenditure against either revenue or capital employed.	
(c)	The financial stability of a business on a short-term basis.	
(d)	The effective and efficient use of assets and liabilities.	

7. Marina has recently won some money and she has decided to invest in one of two companies. Marina has decided to calculate financial ratios based on the information from the financial statements she has received about the two companies.

Discuss the limitations of using financial ratios to make this investment decision.

8. The financial statements for Calvin Ltd for the last two years are as follows:

Calvin Ltd

Income Statement for the year ended 30 April 20-8

	20-8		20-7	
	£000	£000	£000	£000
Revenue		10,800		5,600
Opening inventory	652		350	
Purchases	7,994		3,942	
	8,646		4,292	
Less Closing inventory	654		652	
Cost of sales		7,992		3,640
Gross profit		2,808		1,960
Less Expenses:				
Administration expenses	1,202		813	
Distribution expenses	120		65	
		1,322		878
Profit for the year from operations		1,486		1,082
Less Finance costs		190		18
Profit for the year before tax		1,296		1,064
Less Tax		260		210
Profit for the year after tax		1,036		854

Calvin Ltd
Statement of Financial Position as at 30 April 20-8

	20-8		20-7	
	£000	£000	£000	£000
Non-current assets				
Plant and equipment		1,050		1,100
Current assets				
Inventory	654		652	
Trade receivables	2,850		950	
Cash and equivalents	–		780	
		3,504		2,382
TOTAL ASSETS		4,554		3,482
EQUITY				
Ordinary shares		1,200		1,200
Retained earnings		156		837
TOTAL EQUITY		1,356		2,037
Non-current liabilities				
Loans		498		805
Current liabilities				
Bank overdraft	690		–	
Trade payables	1,750		430	
Tax liability	260		210	
		2,700		640
		4,554		3,482

Required:

Calculate the following ratios for the year ended 30 April 20-8 for Calvin Ltd in the table below (the ones for the previous year have already been entered):

Ratio	30 April 20-8	30 April 20-7
Gross profit margin		35%
Profit in relation to revenue		19%
Return on capital employed		38.07%
Interest cover		60.11 times
Current ratio		3.72 : 1
Liquid capital ratio		2.7 : 1
Trade receivables days		61.92 days
Trade payable days		39.81 days
Rate of inventory turnover days		50.24 days
Capital gearing		28.33%

Workings:

9. Mike is considering investing in Calvin Ltd. Using the financial statements and the ratios you calculated in the previous question, along with the ratios from the previous year, write a report to Mike recommending whether or not he should invest in Calvin Ltd.

REPORT	
To:	Mike
From:	AQA accounting student
Subject:	Potential investment in Calvin Ltd
Date:	Today

10. Turkish Baths plc made a profit from operations of £3,860,000 in the year ended 31 March 20-8, however the statement of financial position shows that the bank account at the start of the year was £625,000 and at the end of the year was overdrawn by £107,000.

Ian, a shareholder, would like an explanation of the reasons for the difference between the two figures and has supplied you with the statement of cash flows below:

Turkish Baths plc
Statement of Cash Flows for the year ended 31 March 20-8

	£000	£000
Profit from operations		3,860
Depreciation		516
Increase in inventory		(502)
Increase in trade receivables		(368)
Increase in trade payables		31
Cash from operating activities		**3,537**
Interest paid		(31)
Tax paid		(740)
Net cash from operating activities		**2,766**
Investing activities		
Purchase of non-current assets	(2,584)	
Net cash used in investing activities		**(2,584)**
Financing activities		
Decrease in non-current loans	(580)	
Dividends paid	(334)	
Net cash used in financing activities		**(914)**
Net decrease in cash and cash equivalents		**(732)**
Cash and cash equivalents at the start of the year		625
Cash and cash equivalents at the end of the year		(107)

Required:

Explain to Ian the differences between profit from operations and the fall in the bank balance of Turkish Baths plc for the year ended 31 March 20-8.

CHAPTER 9: ACCOUNTING REGULATIONS AND ETHICS

1. The legal and regulatory framework of the accounting sector includes:

		True	False
(a)	Accounting standards		
(b)	Company law		
(c)	UK's Corporate Governance Code		
(d)	Conceptual Framework for Financial Reporting		

2. An office junior has told a partner that she can prepare payroll records for a client. You know that she is related to the director of the client company.

   The fundamental principle of ethical behaviour threatened by this situation is:

A	Integrity	
B	Objectivity	
C	Professional competence and due care	
D	Professional behaviour	

3. Sam has worked in practice for many years, however, he is not familiar with the law relating to insolvency and has consulted a legal expert about a specific client.

   This is an example of:

A	Integrity	
B	Confidentiality	
C	Professional competence and due care	
D	Objectivity	

4. An accountant has prepared the financial statements of a limited company who employs him. The managing director has told the accountant, "unless you increase the figure for purchases, your job will be on the line".

   This is an example of:

A	a self-interest threat	
B	an intimidation threat	
C	a self-review threat	
D	a familiarity threat	

5. The Consultative Committee of Accountancy Bodies (CCAB) includes:

A	Her Majesty's Revenue and Customs (HMRC)	
B	Financial Reporting Council (FRC)	
C	Association of Chartered Certified Accountants (ACCA)	
D	Chartered Institute of Management Accountants (CIMA)	

6. State three safeguards which have been introduced by the accountancy profession, legislation or accountancy regulations to guard against threats to fundamental ethical principles.

7. List two examples of Corporate Social Responsibility policies a large company may wish to adopt.

8. Explain the steps that an accountant in practice should take to deal with unethical or illegal acts committed by a client.

MANAGEMENT ACCOUNTING

QUESTIONS

CHAPTER 10: MANAGEMENT ACCOUNTING: THE USE OF BUDGETS

1. From the statements below identify which ones relate to management accounting:

(a)	Reports are in a set format which are often required by law.	
(b)	Reports are based on the recent past and projections for the future.	
(c)	Reports are produced to aid decision making, planning and control.	
(d)	Reports are used primarily for internal purposes.	

2. Select the correct definition of a budget from the statements below:

(a)	The difference between expected and actual revenues or costs.	
(b)	The period of time it takes for the initial cost of an investment to be repaid from net cash inflows.	
(c)	A financial plan for a business which is prepared in advance and generally covers a period of up to 12 months.	
(d)	A costing method which identifies what causes overheads to be incurred.	

3. The following information is available from Sheffield Steel Ltd, a manufacturer of steel rods:

	Month 1 (units)	Month 2 (units)
Sales	6,240	7,860
Opening inventory	1,560	

The closing inventory should be maintained at 25% of the following month's sales.

The production budget for month 1 is:

A	5,835 units	
B	4,680 units	
C	8,205 units	
D	6,645 units	

4. Hippy Ltd started to trade on 1 July and has the following budgeted credit purchases:

July	£21,000
August	£23,000

50% of trade payables will be paid in the month of purchase and a 2% cash discount will be deducted.

The remainder of trade payables will be paid in the month after purchase, with no cash discount.

The amount to be paid in August to trade payables is:

A	£22,540	
B	£21,770	
C	£22,000	
D	£21,560	

5. Each unit of product S requires 3.5 labour hours.

   The number of units of product S required to be produced in May is 300.

   There are 1,000 labour hours available for product S in May.

   Calculate the surplus or shortfall of labour hours for the month of May for product S.

6. Beverley Ltd sells memory sticks at a unit price of £15.50. The sales manager has predicted sales for the next six months to be:

January	800 units
February	As January with a 10% increase
March	As January with a 10% increase
April	As March with a 5% decrease
May	As January
June	As May with a 15% increase

    Calculate the sales units and sales values for memory sticks for the next six months and enter them into the table below.

	Jan	Feb	Mar	Apr
Units				
	£	£	£	£
Sales				

	May	Jun	Total
Units			
	£	£	£
Sales			

7. The following budgeted information is available about product C34:

- Standard material usage per unit is 3 kg.
- Budgeted sales per month:

Month 1	500 units
Month 2	600 units
Month 3	560 units
Month 4	650 units
Month 5	600 units

- Opening inventory at the start of month 1 of finished units is 125.
- Each month's closing inventory of finished units is to be 25% of the following month's sales, however, the maximum capacity in the warehouse is 160 units.
- Opening inventory at the start of month 1 of materials is 315 kg.
- Each month's closing inventory of materials is to be maintained at one fifth of the following month's production.
- The required materials for production in month 5 is estimated at 1,830 kg.
- The cost per kg of material is £0.50.

Complete the table on the following page to calculate the cost of material purchases for product C34 for months 1 to 4.

Solution:

Production budget (units):

	Month 1	Month 2	Month 3	Month 4
Sales	500	600	560	650
Closing inventory	150	140	160	150
Less opening inventory	(125)	(150)	(140)	(160)
Production (units)	525	590	580	640

Material purchases budget (kg):

	Month 1	Month 2	Month 3	Month 4
Materials required for production (kg)	1,575	1,770	1,740	1,920
Closing inventory	354	348	384	366
Less opening inventory	(315)	(354)	(348)	(384)
Purchases (kg)	1,614	1,764	1,776	1,902
Cost of purchases @ £0.50/kg	£807	£882	£888	£951

	Month 1	Month 2	Month 3	Month 4
Production budget	Units	Units	Units	Units
Sales				
Opening inventory				
Closing inventory				
Production				
Purchases budget	kg	kg	kg	kg
Production				
Opening inventory				
Closing inventory				
Purchases				
Purchases budget	£	£	£	£
Purchases				

Workings:

8. Sis Ltd makes sales to its customers on credit. The following information is available for April to June:

- Budgeted credit sales:

    April   £30,000

    May   £37,500

    June   £45,000

- 40% of trade receivables pay in the month of sale, taking advantage of a 3% cash discount which is available.

- The remainder of trade receivables pay in the following month and do not receive a cash discount. However, 5% of these will never pay and should be regarded as irrecoverable debts.

- Trade receivables at 1 April are £16,800.

Complete the table below to calculate receipts from trade receivables for April to June for Sis Ltd:

	April	May	June
Receipts:	£	£	£
Month of sale			
Less Discount			
Month after sale			
Less Irrecoverable debts			
Total			

Workings:

9. Alistair runs a business called 'The IT Shop' and is considering expanding. He has asked you to produce a cash budget for the next three months based on his plan and has provided the following information:

- The bank balance at 1 January 20-8 is £5,866.

- Budgeted sales for the next three months are:

	Cash (£)	Credit (£)
January	1,500	23,000
February	1,600	24,000
March	1,650	26,000

- 30% of credit customers pay in the month of sale, taking advantage of a 3% cash discount which is available.

- 40% of credit customers pay in the month after sale, with the remainder paying in the following month.

- Trade receivables at 1 January 20-8 are:

	£	
November sales	4,800	
December sales	11,900	(£6,800 is expected in January)
Total	16,700	

- All purchases are made on credit and paid for in the following month, purchases forecasts are:

	£
January	5,750
February	6,000
March	6,500

- Trade payables at 1 January 20-8 are £4,250.

- The cost of a major shop refit is £28,000 and this will be paid for in February.

- Operating expenses total £3,600 per month and Alistair's drawings are £1,800 per month; both are paid for in the month they are incurred.

(a) Prepare a cash budget for 'The IT Shop' for the period ended 31 March 20-8:

	January	February	March
	£	£	£

(b) Alistair has an existing overdraft agreement with the bank for £1,000. He would like to know whether he should apply to the bank for an increase in the limit.

Based on the cash budget you have prepared, advise Alistair on whether he needs to increase his overdraft limit.

10. Further information about 'The IT Shop' is:

- Opening inventory at 1 January 20-8 is £1,684.
- Closing inventory at 31 March 20-8 is estimated to be £2,400.
- Non-current assets at 1 January 20-8 are £5,000.
- The depreciation charge for the three months ended 31 March 20-8 is estimated to be £1,500 (this includes the charge for the shop refit).
- Opening capital at 1 January 20-8 is £25,000.

Required:

Prepare the budgeted income statement and budgeted statement of financial position of 'The IT Shop' for the period ended 31 March 20-8, based on the above information and the figures provided and calculated in question 9.

CHAPTER 11: ABSORPTION AND ACTIVITY BASED COSTING

1. Select the correct definition of a cost centre from the statements below:

(a)	Units of output to which costs can be charged.	
(b)	Groups of overhead costs that are incurred by the same activity.	
(c)	Sections of a business to which costs can be charged.	
(d)	Activities which cause costs to be incurred.	

2. From the statements below select whether they relate to marginal, absorption or activity based costing:

Statements		Marginal	Absorption	Activity based
(a)	Overheads are attributed to production on the basis of activities.			
(b)	Costs are classified as either fixed or variable.			
(c)	The overhead absorption rate is usually calculated using direct labour hours or machine hours.			
(d)	The cost of producing one extra unit of output can be identified.			

3. The following information is available about product X:

	£
Total direct material cost	450
Total direct labour cost	510
Overheads	480

150 units of product X are produced.

The absorption cost of producing one unit of product X is:

A	£3.20	
B	£6.20	
C	£6.40	
D	£9.60	

4. The following information is available about product Y:

Selling price per unit	£12.00
Direct material per unit	£2.25
Direct labour per unit	£1.50
Total fixed production overhead	£50,000
Number of units	20,000

The marginal cost of producing one unit of product Y is:

A	£3.75	
B	£5.75	
C	£6.25	
D	£8.25	

5. The following information is available about product Z:

Selling price per unit	£100
Variable cost per unit	£45
Total fixed costs	£88,000
Budgeted production	2,400 units

    How many units of Product Z must be sold to produce a profit of £22,000?

A	880 units	
B	1,100 units	
C	1,600 units	
D	2,000 units	

6. Alpha Kite Ltd uses cost-plus pricing to calculate the selling prices of its products, based on a 25% mark-up on absorption cost.

    The following information is available about product D11:

Prime cost per unit	£360
Fixed overhead per unit	£40

    The selling price per unit of product D11 should be set at:

A	£450	
B	£480	
C	£500	
D	£534	

7. Alpine Coatings Ltd manufactures two products, the Honey Dew and the Sunflower.

The following information is available about the two products:

	Honey Dew	Sunflower
Selling price per unit	£18.00	£22.50
Direct material per unit	£7.40	£8.50
Direct labour per unit	£1.80	£3.60
Monthly production	4,000 units	6,000 units

Alpine Coatings Ltd's total monthly factory overheads are £80,000 and activity based costing is used to absorb the overheads, using the information below:

Cost pool	Overhead per month	Cost driver	Details for each product
Machinery set-ups	£66,000	Number of times machinery is set-up during production	Honey Dew – 3 set-ups per unit produced Sunflower – 8 set-ups per unit produced
Quality inspections	£14,000	Number of times products are inspected during production	Honey Dew – 1 inspection per unit produced Sunflower – 4 inspections per unit produced

Calculate the cost per unit and the profit or loss per unit for each product.

8. State one benefit and one limitation of using marginal, absorption or activity based costing:

	Benefit	**Limitation**
Marginal costing		
Absorption costing		
Activity based costing		

CHAPTER 12: OVERHEADS AND OVERHEAD ABSORPTION

1. Select the correct definition of an indirect cost from the following:

(a)	The cost of producing one extra unit of output.	
(b)	A cost which is shared amongst cost units, as it does not relate to one unit of output.	
(c)	The total budgeted cost of producing one unit of output.	
(d)	The total direct materials and direct labour cost of a unit of output.	

2. The following information is available about a cost centre:

	Budgeted	Actual
Overheads	£500,000	£600,000
Activity	10,000 hours	12,500 hours

The overhead absorption rate for the cost centre is:

A	£40 per hour	
B	£48 per hour	
C	£50 per hour	
D	£60 per hour	

3. MI Ltd operates a system of absorption costing.

Canteen overhead costs are apportioned to departments on the basis of the number of employees in each department, which are:

Production   28
Assembly   52
Finance   8
Administration   12

The canteen overhead costs for the next year are forecast to be £61,000.

How much of the canteen overhead costs will be apportioned to the assembly department?

A	£17,080	
B	£21,350	
C	£31,720	
D	£39,650	

4. The budgeted overhead and activity levels for Bedford Shoes Ltd are:

Department	Production	Packing
Budgeted overhead	£80,000	£43,200
Budgeted direct labour hours	2,500 hours	3,600 hours
Budgeted machine hours	4,000 hours	2,880 hours

Calculate the budgeted overhead absorption rates for each department on the assumption that the processes are heavily automated.

Select the two correct answers:

A	Production – £20 per hour	
B	Production – £32 per hour	
C	Packing – £12 per hour	
D	Packing – £15 per hour	

5. Overheads have been allocated and apportioned to the departments of Pentack Ltd as follows:

Department	Overhead (£)
Production 1	35,100
Production 2	26,700
Production 3	33,200
Maintenance	28,500

The maintenance department overheads are to be re-apportioned to the production departments based on the value of machinery, which is:

Department	Value of machinery (£)
Production 1	560,000
Production 2	490,000
Production 3	350,000
Total	1,400,000

The total overhead allocated to production department 2 after the maintenance department's overheads have been re-apportioned, to the nearest whole £, is:

A	£36,675	
B	£40,325	
C	£45,075	
D	£46,500	

6. Department F3 uses machine hours to calculate the overhead absorption rate and has the following information available for the month:

Overhead absorption rate	£9.20
Actual machine hours for the month	18,375 hours
Actual overhead for the month	£167,285

(a) Calculate the under or over absorption of overhead for the month, clearly stating if it is under or over absorbed.

(b) Suggest an alternative overhead absorption rate department F3 could use and state the circumstances that would make it a more appropriate method.

7. Constantine Hairdressing Ltd has two revenue earning departments; hair and beauty, and one non-revenue earning department; administration.

Budgeted overheads for the next year are:

	£
Supervisor's salary – hair	35,665
Supervisor's salary – beauty	32,135
Receptionist's salary	17,500
Administration salaries	48,000
Rent and rates	50,000
Buildings insurance	15,000
Equipment depreciation	9,000
Equipment insurance	6,000
Total overheads	213,300

The following information is also available:

	Hair	Beauty	Admin.
Floor area (square metres)	240	150	110
Carrying amount of equipment	£18,000	£24,750	£2,250
Use of receptionist's time	60%	40%	–
Chargeable labour hours for the year	8,500	5,200	–

The administration department's overheads are re-apportioned to the revenue earning departments as follows:

Hair   70%

Beauty   30%

(a) Allocate and apportion the overheads to the three departments, using the table on the next page.

(b) Re-apportion the administration department's overheads to the hair and beauty departments, using the table on the next page.

(c) Calculate the overhead absorption rates for the hair and beauty departments, on the basis of chargeable labour hours for the year.

Overheads	Basis of apportionment	Total overheads £	Hair £	Beauty £	Admin. £
Supervisor's salary – hair					
Supervisor's salary – beauty					
Receptionist's salary					
Administration salaries					
Rent and rates					
Buildings insurance					
Equipment depreciation					
Equipment insurance					
Total overheads (a)					
Re-apportion administration					
Total overheads (b)					

(c) Overhead absorption rates:

CHAPTER 13: STANDARD COSTING AND VARIANCE ANALYSIS

Use the following information which is available about product K12 to answer questions 1 and 2:

Standard selling price per unit	£12
Budgeted sales	1,200 units
Actual sales	1,400 units
Actual sales revenue	£15,200

1. The sales volume variance is:

A	£1,600 Adv	
B	£1,600 Fav	
C	£2,400 Adv	
D	£2,400 Fav	

2. The sales price variance is:

A	£1,600 Adv	
B	£1,600 Fav	
C	£2,400 Adv	
D	£2,400 Fav	

Use the following information which is available about the labour costs of product S11 to answer questions 3 and 4:

Standard cost   1,000 hours at £22.00 per hour

Actual cost   1,100 hours at £21.50 per hour

3. The labour rate variance is:

A	£550 Adv
B	£550 Fav
C	£2,200 Adv
D	£2,200 Fav

4. The labour efficiency variance is:

A	£550 Adv
B	£550 Fav
C	£2,200 Adv
D	£2,200 Fav

5. From the explanations below, select all the ones that are correct about an adverse variance:

(a)	Actual costs are higher than standard costs.	
(b)	Actual costs are lower than standard costs.	
(c)	Actual revenue is higher than standard revenue.	
(d)	Actual revenue is lower than standard revenue.	

6. What could cause a favourable materials usage variance from the list below?

(a)	A decrease in shipping costs from materials brought in from overseas.	
(b)	A discount received from a supplier for buying in bulk.	
(c)	The use of higher skilled staff in the production line.	
(d)	Changing to a cheaper material of inferior quality.	

7. The following information is available about the material costs of product D13:

Standard cost   580 kg at £10.50 per kg

Actual cost   560 kg at £11.75 per kg

Calculate the following variances and suggest possible reasons for their causes:

(a) Materials

(b) Materials price

(c) Materials usage

8. Slaveli and Co Consultants work on management projects and operate a standard costing system.

The managing partner is concerned that last month more projects were completed than anticipated, but the actual profit of £36,060 was less than the budgeted profit of £38,000.

The accountant has provided the following information for last month:

	Budget	Actual
Sales	80 projects at £1,200 each	90 projects at £1,150 each
Labour	10 hours per project at £35 per hour	13 hours per project at £32 per hour
Overheads	£30,000	£30,000

The accountant has also calculated the variances as follows:

Variance £
Sales price   4,500 Adv
Sales volume   12,000 Fav
Labour rate   3,510 Fav
Labour efficiency   9,450 Adv

Required:

(a) Prepare a reconciliation statement, which shows how the variances have caused the reduction in profit.

(b) Suggest possible reasons for the variances.

CHAPTER 14: CAPITAL INVESTMENT APPRAISAL

Use the following information to answer questions 1 and 2.

Deborah Groundwork Ltd is considering investing in new machinery at a cost of £700,000 for work on a potential project. Further details about the project are:

Year	Net cash inflow/(outflow)	Discount factor
	£	at 10%
1	(100,000)	0.909
2	600,000	0.826
3	850,000	0.751
4	250,000	0.683

1. The payback period of the project is:

A	1 year 61 days	
B	1 year 73 days	
C	2 years 86 days	
D	2 years 169 days	

2. The net present value of the project is:

A	£513,800	
B	£818,100	
C	£900,000	
D	£1,213,800	

3. From the statements below, select the correct definition of net present value:

(a)	The length of time it takes for the initial cost of a project to be repaid from the net cash inflows.	
(b)	The expected duration of a project.	
(c)	The total discounted cash inflows and cash outflows of a project.	
(d)	The expected rate of return of a project.	

4. Discuss one benefit and one limitation of using the payback method in capital investment decisions.

5. Fierce Construction Ltd is considering investing in a large housing development project.

Suggest two financial factors and two non-financial factors Fierce Construction Ltd should consider before undertaking the project.

6. Safety Watches Ltd is considering developing an App, for which a return of 10% is required. The following information is available about the project:

	Year 0	Year 1	Year 2	Year 3	Year 4	Year 5
	£	£	£	£	£	£
Development costs	88,000	–	–	–	–	–
Sales revenue	–	76,000	160,000	174,000	204,000	54,000
Variable costs	–	38,000	80,000	87,000	102,000	27,000
Fixed costs	–	15,000	15,000	15,000	15,000	15,000
10% discount factor	1.0	0.909	0.826	0.751	0.683	0.621

(a) Calculate the payback of the project.

(b) Calculate the net present value of the project.

7. The directors of Nottingsham Sports Ltd are considering two alternative investment projects. Whichever project is chosen, the company will have to borrow the initial investment at a variable interest rate of 5% per annum.

   Project X involves the conversion of a local village community shop and café, which is run by volunteers, into a branded sports shop, which will be run by trained specialist staff from outside the area. The current shop is thriving, but continually makes a loss.

   Project Y involves extending a sports pavilion in a deprived community. The extension will include changing and sports facilities for both women and people with disabilities, as the current pavilion only has a male changing room. The project will involve creating up to five jobs for people from the local community.

   The accountant of Nottingsham Sports Ltd has carried out investment appraisals on both projects which is as follows:

	Project X	Project Y
Initial investment	£50,000	£100,000
Net present value	£70,000	£140,000
Payback period	3 years	2 years
Estimated life of the project	10 years	7 years

   The net present value was calculated using a discount rate of 8% for both projects. This was based on the current return on capital employed of 3%, plus the interest rate of 5%.

   Assess the two projects and recommend to the directors of Nottingsham Sports Ltd the one they should accept.

Answers

Financial Accounting page 106

Management Accounting page 148

FINANCIAL ACCOUNTING
ANSWERS

CHAPTER 1: FINANCIAL STATEMENTS AND INTRODUCTION TO ETHICS

1. (a) and (d) relate to financial accounting.

   (b) and (c) relate to management accounting.

2. C

3. A

4. C

   (£11,325 − £1,065) × 5% = £513.

5.

Oliver Limited

Income Statement for the year ended 31 May 20-8

	£000	£000
Revenue		3,803
Opening inventory	75	
Purchases	2,438	
	2,513	
Less Closing inventory	79	
Cost of sales		2,434
Gross profit		1,369
Less Expenses:		
Administration expenses	485	
Distribution expenses	79	
		564
Profit for the year from operations		805
Less Finance costs		27
Profit for the year before tax		778
Less Tax		162
Profit for the year after tax		616

Statement of Changes in Equity for the year ended 31 May 20-8

	Share capital £000	Share premium £000	Retained earnings £000	Total £000
Balances at start	400	100	577	1,077
Profit for the year			616	616
Dividends paid			(236)	(236)
Balances at end	400	100	957	1,457

Statement of Financial Position as at 31 May 20-8

	£000 Cost	£000 Depreciation	£000 Carrying amount
Non-current assets			
Plant and equipment	2,160	757	1,403
Current assets			
Inventory		79	
Trade and other receivables		610	
Cash and cash equivalents		207	
		896	
Less Current liabilities			
Trade and other payables	215		
Tax liabilities	162		
		377	
Net Current assets			519
			1,922
Less Non-current liabilities			465
NET ASSETS			1,457
EQUITY			
Ordinary shares			400
Share premium			100
Retained earnings			957
TOTAL EQUITY			1,457

CHAPTER 2: INCOMPLETE RECORDS

1. £19,500

    (£4,000 + £15,000 + £6,500 + £3,600 – £1,400 – £8,200)

2. B

    (£16,800 + £5,100 – £9,700 = £12,200)

3. £10,590

Dr			Bank account		Cr
20-8		£	20-8		£
31 Dec	Capital introduced	10,000	31 Dec	Trade payables	26,510
31 Dec	Trade receivables	48,900	31 Dec	Fixtures and fittings	14,000
			31 Dec	Drawings	7,800
			31 Dec	**Balance c/d**	**10,590**
		58,900			58,900
20-9			20-9		
1 Jan	Balance b/d	10,590			

4. D

Dr		Purchases ledger control account			Cr
20-7/8		£	20-7/8		£
30 Nov	Bank payments	147,300	1 Dec	Balance b/d	13,800
30 Nov	Purchases returns	438	**30 Nov**	**Purchases (Bal.)**	**151,273**
30 Nov	Discounts received	1,685			
30 Nov	Balance c/d	15,650			
		165,073			165,073
20-8/9			20-8/9		
			1 Dec	Balance b/d	15,650

5. A

Dr		Wages account			Cr
20-7/8		£	20-7/8		£
31 Aug	**Bank payments (Bal.)**	**56,200**	1 Sep	Balance b/d	600
31 Aug	Balance c/d	900	31 Aug	Income statement	56,500
		57,100			57,100
20-8/9			20-8/9		
			1 Sep	Balance b/d	900

6. D

Dr	Disposals account		Cr
	£		£
Cost	22,000	Depreciation	14,000
Profit on sale	3,000	**Sale proceeds (Bal.)**	**11,000**
	25,000		25,000

7. £350,000

    (£500,000 × (100% − 30%))

8. C

	£	£	%
Revenue		200,000	125
Opening inventory	15,000		
Purchases (Bal.)	**165,000**		
	180,000		
Less Closing inventory	(20,000)		
Cost of sales		160,000	100
Gross profit		40,000	25

9. £750

Dr	Cash account		Cr
	£		£
Balance b/d	450	Bankings	46,200
Takings	54,600	Cash payments	7,600
		Cash Stolen (Bal.)	**750**
		Balance c/d	500
	55,050		55,050

10.

(a) £74,418 (£14,250 – £5,600 + £56,800 + £8,968 (opening bank))

(b) **Bernard**

Trading section of Income Statement for the year ended 31 December 20-8

	£	£
Revenue (W1)		339,018
Opening inventory	14,250	
Purchases (W2)	232,934	
	247,184	
Less Goods for own use (W4)	2,262	
	244,922	
Less Closing inventory	18,910	
Cost of sales		226,012
Gross profit (W3)		**113,006**

W1   Revenue £336,236 + £2,782 = £339,018

W2   Purchases

Dr	Purchases ledger control account		Cr
	£		£
Bank	225,724	Balance b/d	5,600
Bank	4,960	Purchases (Bal.)	**232,934**
Balance c/d	7,850		
	238,534		238,534

W3   Gross profit £339,018 × 50%/150% = £113,006

W4   Cost of sales £339,018 − £113,006 = £226,012

Goods taken for own use £226,012 + £18,910 − £232,934 − £14,250 = £2,262

(c) **Bernard**

Income Statement for the year ended 31 December 20-8

	£	£
Gross profit		113,006
Less Expenses:		
Rent (W5)	12,000	
Loss on sale of equipment (W6)	520	
Depreciation (W7)	13,900	
General expenses	15,326	
Wages	44,000	
		85,746
Net profit for the year		27,260

W5   Rent £11,000 + £1,000 = £12,000

W6   Loss on sale of equipment

Dr	Disposals account		Cr
	£		£
Carrying value	1,200	Sale proceeds	680
		Loss on sale (Bal.)	**520**
	1,200		1,200

W7 Depreciation

Dr	Shop equipment		Cr
	£		£
Balance b/d	56,800	Disposal	1,200
		Depreciation (Bal.)	**13,900**
		Balance c/d	41,700
	56,800		56,800

(d) **Bernard**

Statement of Financial Position as at 31 December 20-8

	£	£	£
Non-current assets			
Shop equipment			41,700
Current assets			
Inventory		18,910	
Bank (W8)		5,656	
		24,566	
Less Current liabilities			
Trade payables	7,850		
Other payables	1,000		
		8,850	
Net current assets			15,716
NET ASSETS			57,416
FINANCED BY			
Opening capital			74,418
Add Profit for the year			27,260
			101,678
Less Drawings (W9)			44,262
			57,416

W8 Bank £7,834 – £4,960 + £2,782 = £5,656

W9 Drawings £42,000 + £2,262 (goods for own use) = £44,262

CHAPTER 3: COMPUTER ACCOUNTING

1. (a), (c) and (d) are advantages.

   (b) is a disadvantage.

2. The costs that could be incurred include:

   - the initial capital cost of the hardware and software, including installation costs
   - ongoing costs relating to software, such as replacements, updating and support
   - costs associated with disruption while the new system is installed, this may include staff overtime and IT specialists and the costs of running both the old and new systems for a period of time
   - staff training costs
   - there may be staff redundancies
   - back up and security, the costs associated with ensuring that data is backed up and secure at all times.

3. Disadvantages include any two from the following list:

Disadvantages	Explanation
cost	the capital costs of hardware and software and the costs of training, maintenance and updating
staff opposition	some employees may not like computers and some jobs may be lost as manual processes are automated
system failure	if software crashes or hardware fails, there will be disruption to the workflow and in a worst-case scenario, loss of data which may not have been backed up
errors	although data entry is made simpler with a computer based system, errors can still occur and go undetected

security	there is always the danger of the system being hacked, viruses entering a system and risk of data theft by staff
health and safety	the increasing use of computers at work may aggravate the problems of bad backs, eyestrain and muscular complaints

4. **Benefits** of spreadsheets include:

- **speed**

    the use of formulae enables figures to be changed and the results seen immediately

- **ease of use**

    a correctly set up spreadsheet will allow users to input data easily

- **output**

    printouts and reports can be produced easily.

    Drawbacks of spreadsheets include:

- **inaccurate information**

    formulae may be set up incorrectly, therefore the information produced may be inaccurate

- **security**

    if passwords and restricted access to use are not in place, data may be accidentally or intentionally altered

- **corruption**

    data may become corrupted and therefore potentially lost

- **back up**

    correct back up procedures must be in place, there is a danger of a spreadsheet being out of date or two users using different versions of the same file.

CHAPTER 4: PARTNERSHIP FINANCIAL STATEMENTS

1. (a), (b) and (c) are false.

   (d) is true.

2. B

   ((£12,000 × 5%) + £53,400) ÷ 2 = £27,000

3. A

Dr	Current account – Margaret		Cr
	£		£
Drawings	15,000	Salary	16,000
Interest on drawings	300	Interest on capital	2,250
Balance c/d (Bal.)	**21,950**	Share of profit	19,000
	37,250		37,250

4.

Alison, Bernadette and Coleen

Profit appropriation account for the year ended 31 March 20-8

	£	£
Profit for the year		66,500
Less appropriation of profit:		
Salary:		
Alison	10,000	
Coleen	20,000	
		30,000
Interest on capital:		
Alison (£10,000 × 3%)	300	
Bernadette (£30,000 × 3%)	900	
Coleen (£10,000 × 3%)	300	
		1,500
		35,000
Share of remaining profit		
Alison (£35,000 × 30%)	10,500	
Bernadette (£35,000 × 50%)	17,500	
Coleen (£35,000 × 20%)	7,000	
		35,000

5.

Dr				Capital accounts				Cr
20-8		Eliza	Sam	20-8		Eliza	Sam
		£	£			£	£
				1 Jan	Balance b/d	40,000	30,000
31 Dec	Balance c/d	40,000	30,000				
		40,000	30,000			40,000	30,000
20-9				20-9			
				1 Jan	Balance b/d	40,000	30,000

Dr				Current accounts			Cr
20-8		Eliza	Sam	20-8		Eliza	Sam
		£	£			£	£
1 Jan	Balance b/d	480		1 Jan	Balance b/d		1,310
31 Dec	Drawings	12,000	28,640	31 Dec	Salary	8,000	
31 Dec	Interest on drawings	600	1,432	31 Dec	Interest on capital	2,400	1,800
				31 Dec	Share of profit (W1)	18,660	12,440
31 Dec	Balance c/d	15,980		31 Dec	Balance c/d		14,522
		29,060	30,072			29,060	30,072
20-9				20-9			
1 Jan	Balance b/d		14,522	1 Jan	Balance b/d	15,980	

W1   Share of profit £41,268 + £600 + £1,432 − £8,000 − £2,400 − £1,800 = £31,100

Eliza £31,100 × 60% = £18,660, Sam £31,100 × 40% = £12,440

6. Obscure Fiction partnership

Income Statement for the year ended 31 March 20-8

	£	£
Revenue		79,800
Opening inventory	5,865	
Purchases	36,750	
	42,615	
Less Closing inventory	6,273	
Cost of sales		36,342
Gross profit		43,458
Add: Discounts received		524
Less Expenses:		
Wages (W1)	7,436	
Rent and rates (W2)	7,800	
Sundry expenses	585	
Credit card charges	880	
Motor expenses	689	
Depreciation (W3)	6,200	
		23,590
Profit for the year		20,392

W1 Wages £7,380 + £56 = £7,436

W2 Rent and rates £8,300 − £500 = £7,800

W3 Depreciation £24,800 × 25% = £6,200

Dr				Capital accounts			Cr	
20-7/8		Ayesha	Josh	20-7/8			Ayesha	Josh
		£	£				£	£
				1 Apr	Balance b/d		25,000	25,000
31 Mar	Balance c/d	25,000	25,000					
		25,000	25,000				25,000	25,000
20-8				20-8				
				1 Apr	Balance b/d		25,000	25,000

Dr				Current accounts			Cr	
20-7/8		Ayesha	Josh	20-7/8			Ayesha	Josh
		£	£				£	£
1 Apr	Balance b/d	450		1 Apr	Balance b/d			180
31 Mar	Drawings	6,845	13,050	31 Mar	Salary			6,000
				31 Mar	Interest on capital (W4)		1,250	1,250
				31 Mar	Share of profit (W5)		5,946	5,946
31 Mar	Balance c/d		326	31 Mar	Balance c/d		99	
		7,295	13,376				7,295	13,376
20-8				20-8				
1 Apr	Balance b/d	99		1 Apr	Balance b/d			326

W4 Interest on capital £25,000 × 5% = £1,250 each

W5 Share of profit £20,392 − £6,000 − £1,250 − £1,250 = £11,892 ÷ 2 = £5,946

Obscure Fiction partnership
Statement of Financial Position as at 31 March 20-8

	£ Cost	£ Depreciation	£ Carrying amount
Non-current assets			
Equipment	24,800	6,200	18,600
Current assets			
Inventory		6,273	
Other receivables		500	
Bank		27,800	
		34,573	
Less Current liabilities			
Trade payables	2,890		
Other payables	56		
		2,946	
Net current assets			31,627
NET ASSETS			50,227
FINANCED BY:			
Capital accounts:			
Ayesha			25,000
Josh			25,000
			50,000
Current accounts:			
Ayesha		(99)	
Josh		326	227
TOTAL EQUITY			50,227

CHAPTER 5: CHANGES IN PARTNERSHIPS

1. (c)

2. D

Dr Goodwill, Cr Capital accounts (old profit sharing ratio), Clive is £10,000 (£50,000 × 20%)

Cr Goodwill, Dr Capital accounts (new profit sharing ratio), Clive is £20,000 (£50,000 × 40%)

3. B

Dr		Capital account – Donald		Cr
	£			£
Bank	50,000	Balance b/d		30,000
Loan (Bal.)	25,000	Share of goodwill		45,000
	75,000			75,000

4.

Dr				Capital accounts				Cr
	D	E	F		D	E	F
	£	£	£		£	£	£
Share of goodwill	38,400	12,800	12,800	Balance b/d	30,000	30,000	
				Bank			50,000
				Share of goodwill	32,000	32,000	
Balance c/d	31,400	57,000	37,200	Reval.	7,800	7,800	
	69,800	69,800	50,000		69,800	69,800	50,000
				Balance b/d	31,400	57,000	37,200

5. 'IT for Novices'

Partnership appropriation account for the year ended 31 December 20-8

	Three months ended 31 March 20-8 £	Nine months ended 31 December 20-8 £	Total £
Profit for the year	30,000	90,000	120,000
Less appropriation of profit:			
Salary:			
Xaviar	4,500	13,500	18,000
Yan	6,000	18,000	24,000
Zain	0	9,000	9,000
	10,500	40,500	51,000
Interest on capital:			
Xaviar	240	720	960
Yan	210	630	840
Zain	0	450	450
	450	1,800	2,250
Remaining profit	19,050	47,700	66,750
Share of remaining profit:			
Xaviar	13,335	28,620	41,955
Yan	5,715	9,540	15,255
Zain	0	9,540	9,540
	19,050	47,700	66,750

6. **'Our Local Café' partnership**

Income Statement for the year ended 31 December 20-8

	£	£
Revenue		266,700
Opening inventory	10,200	
Purchases	151,438	
	161,638	
Less Goods for own use	750	
	160,888	
Less Closing inventory	15,300	
Cost of sales		145,588
Gross profit		121,112
Less Expenses:		
Wages	29,200	
Office costs	10,196	
Sundry expenses	1,386	
		40,782
Profit for the year		80,330
Share of profit:		
Peggy (£80,330 × 40%)		32,132
Nora (£80,330 × 40%)		32,132
Queenie (£80,330 × 20%)		16,066
		80,330

Capital accounts

Dr									Cr
20-8		Peggy £	Nora £	Queenie £	20-8		Peggy £	Nora £	Queenie £
1 Jan	Goodwill	26,000	26,000	13,000	1 Jan	Balance b/d	15,000	15,000	
					1 Jan	Bank			44,500
					1 Jan	Revaluation	10,000	10,000	
31 Dec	Balance c/d	31,500	31,500	31,500	1 Jan	Goodwill	32,500	32,500	
		57,500	57,500	44,500			57,500	57,500	44,500
20-9					1 Jan	Balance b/d	31,500	31,500	31,500

Current accounts

Dr									Cr
20-8		Peggy £	Nora £	Queenie £	20-8		Peggy £	Nora £	Queenie £
31 Dec	Drawings	33,000	32,000	17,000	1 Jan	Balance b/d	580	630	
31 Dec	Own use	750			31 Dec	Profit	32,132	32,132	16,066
31 Dec	Balance c/d		762		31 Dec	Balance c/d	1,038		934
		33,750	32,762	17,000			33,750	32,762	17,000
20-9					20-9				
1 Jan	Balance b/d	1,038		934	1 Jan	Balance b/d		762	

'Our Local Café' partnership

Statement of Financial Position as at 31 December 20-8

	£	£	£
Non-current assets			
Property			50,000
Current assets			
Inventory		15,300	
Bank		43,550	
		———	
		58,850	
Less Current liabilities			
Trade payables	15,560		
	———		
		15,560	
		———	
Net current assets			43,290
			———
NET ASSETS			93,290
			———
FINANCED BY:			
Capital accounts:			
Peggy			31,500
Nora			31,500
Queenie			31,500
			———
			94,500
Current accounts:			
Peggy		(1,038)	
Nora		762	
Queenie		(934)	(1,210)
		———	———
TOTAL EQUITY			93,290
			———

CHAPTER 6: ACCOUNTING FOR LIMITED COMPANIES

1. (a), (b), (d), (f) and (h) are true.

    (c), (e) and (g) are false.

2. (d)

3. (a), (b) and (c) are false.

    (d) is true.

4. (a) The responsibilities of directors under the Companies Act 2006 are to:

    - act within their powers in accordance with the company's constitution
    - promote the company's success
    - act independently
    - ensure they take reasonable care and due diligence
    - ensure they have the correct skills
    - avoid conflicts of interest
    - not accept benefits from third parties
    - disclose interests in any proposed transactions involving the company
    - ensure the accounting records and financial statements are properly maintained.

(b) The items which should be contained within the directors' report include:

- the principle activities of the company
- a review of the activities over the last year
- likely future developments that will affect the company
- the names of the directors and their shareholdings
- significant differences in property valuations (book value compared to market value)
- political and charitable donations
- actions taken on employee involvement and consultation
- the company policy on the employment of disabled people
- the company policy on health and safety
- the company policy on the payment of suppliers

5. External stakeholders and their interests include any two from the following:

customers	to ensure goods and services will be available in the future
suppliers	to ensure the company can pay for goods and services supplied
lenders	to view the security available on loans and the company's ability to pay its commitments
government	to ensure taxes are paid and business statistics are collated
local community	to view the contribution the company makes to the economy

Internal stakeholders and their interests include any two from the following:

shareholders	to establish the company's profitability and the dividends paid
management	to see the future prospects of the company
employees	to ensure the company's ability to pay and future employment

6. Benefits of published accounts include any two from the following:

produced annually	reports can be reviewed at least once a year and comparisons made
available to all shareholders	the financial statements must be made available to all shareholders; therefore, performance can be reviewed
filed with Companies House	for private companies the filing deadline is nine months and public companies the filing deadline is six months, this means companies have a time limit for producing the required information
larger companies require an audit	an independent audit is a requirement for larger companies which means that the contents are verified by someone outside of the company
prepared in accordance with the accounting framework	the same legal and accounting standards are followed, which enable comparisons to be made

Limitations of published accounts include any two from the following:

information is out of date	the information is historic and does not show any recent changes that may have occurred
additional information is not disclosed	only the information required by the accounting framework will be included
information gives no indication of future performance	the information gives little indication of what may happen in the future
information is financial only	the information is limited to financial performance only, there is no indication of non-financial performance, such as customer satisfaction or quality control

7. B

200,000 × 4 = 800,000 shares, ÷ 8 = 100,000 new shares, × 50p = £50,000.

Note: The shares are 25p shares, therefore multiply by 4.

8.

Georgie Ltd

Statement of Changes in Equity for the year ended 31 December 20-8

	Share capital £000	Share premium £000	Retained earnings £000	Reval. reserve £000	Total £000
At 1 January 20-8	300	50	41	–	391
Issue of shares (W1)	60	(50)	(10)	–	–
Revaluation	–	–	–	200	200
Profit for the year	–	–	285	–	285
Dividends paid	–	–	(240)	–	(240)
At 31 December 20-8	360	–	76	200	636

W1 Bonus issue £300,000 × 10 (10p shares) = 3,000,000 shares ÷ 5 = 600,000 × 10p = £60,000.

The bonus shares have been issued from the share premium account first, and the remainder from retained earnings.

Note: Only dividends paid are included.

9.   **Fitness plc**

Non-current assets note for the year ended 31 May 20-8

	Land and buildings £000	Plant and equipment £000	Total £000
Cost			
At 1 June 20-7	250	425	675
Additions at cost	–	162	162
Less Cost of disposals	–	(40)	(40)
Revaluation	100	–	100
At 31 May 20-8	**350**	**547**	**897**
Depreciation			
At 1 June 20-7	25	237	262
Charge for the year (W1)	7	80	87
Less Eliminated on disposal	–	(10)	(10)
Less Eliminated on revaluation	(25)	–	(25)
At 31 May 20-8	**7**	**307**	**314**
Carrying amount at 31 May 20-8	**343**	**240**	**583**

W1   Depreciation land and buildings £350,000 × 2% = £7,000

Depreciation plant and equipment (£425,000 + £162,000 – £40,000 – £237,000 + £10,000) × 25% = £80,000

10. Victor Ltd

Income Statement for the year ended 31 March 20-8

	£000	£000
Revenue		1,084
Opening inventory	57	
Purchases	484	
	541	
Less Closing inventory	65	
Cost of sales		476
Gross profit		608
Less Expenses:		
Administration expenses (W1)	223	
Distribution expenses (W2)	197	
		420
Profit for the year from operations		188
Less Finance costs		2
Profit for the year before tax		186
Less Tax		35
Profit for the year after tax		151

W1   Administration expenses

	£000	
Per trial balance	131	
Irrecoverable debts	17	
Depreciation	75	£750,000 × 20% × 50%
	223	

W2   Distribution expenses

	£000	
Per trial balance	122	
Depreciation	75	£750,000 × 20% × 50%
	197	

Victor Ltd

Statement of Changes in Equity for the year ended 31 March 20-8

	Share capital £000	Share premium £000	Retained earnings £000	Reval. reserve £000	Total £000
At 1 April 20-7	300	150	107	–	557
Revaluation	–	–	–	70	70
Profit for the year	–	–	151	–	151
Dividends paid	–	–	(136)	–	(136)
At 31 March 20-8	300	150	122	70	642

Victor Ltd

Statement of Financial Position as at 31 March 20-8

Non-current assets	£000 Cost/ Valuation	£000 Depreciation	£000 Carrying amount
Property	450	–	450
Plant and equipment (W3)	750	635	115
	1,200	635	565

	£000	£000
Current assets		
Inventory	65	
Trade receivables (W4)	177	
	242	
Less Current liabilities		
Bank overdraft	48	
Trade payables	82	
Tax liabilities	35	
	165	
Net current assets		77
NET ASSETS		642

EQUITY	
Ordinary shares	300
Share premium	150
Retained earnings	122
Revaluation reserve	70
TOTAL EQUITY	642

W3 Depreciation plant and equipment £485,000 + £150,000 = £635,000

W4 Trade receivables £194,000 – £17,000 = £177,000

CHAPTER 7: STATEMENT OF CASH FLOWS

1. (c)

2. D

	£
Loss from operations	(6,846)
Depreciation	5,064
Loss on sale of non-current assets	782
Decrease in inventory	2,889
Increase in trade receivables	(3,015)
Increase in trade payables	2,930
Cash from operating activities	**1,804**

3. D

£5,127 + £9,084 = £14,211.

Note: The change in the bank loan is included in financing activities.

4. A

	£
Proceeds from the sale of non-current assets	8,500
Purchase of non-current assets	(86,000)
Dividends received	1,200
Investing activities	**(76,300)**

5. C

	£
Receipts from the issue of share capital	10,250
Increase in non-current loans	6,000
Dividends paid	(15,000)
Financing activities	**1,250**

6.

Purchase of non-current assets = £14,942:

Dr	Property, plant and equipment		Cr
	£		£
Balance b/d	57,248	Depreciation	7,283
Additions (Bal.)	**14,942**	Disposal	1,800
		Balance c/d	63,107
	72,190		72,190

Proceeds from the sale of non-current assets = £2,050:

Dr	Disposals		Cr
	£		£
Property, plant and equip.	1,800	Sale proceeds (Bal.)	**2,050**
Profit on sale	250		
	2,050		2,050

7. Ninety Ltd

Statement of Cash Flows for the year ended 31 December 20-8

	£000	£000
Profit from operations (W1)		1,805
Depreciation		276
Profit on sale of non-current assets (W3)		(3)
Decrease in inventory		11
Increase in trade receivables		(32)
Increase in trade payables		16
Cash from operating activities		**2,073**
Interest paid		(152)
Tax paid		(353)
Net cash from operating activities		**1,568**
Investing activities		
Purchase of non-current assets	(784)	
Proceeds from sale of non-current assets	14	
Net cash used in investing activities		**(770)**
Financing activities		
Receipts from issue of share capital (W4)	230	
Increase in non-current loans	315	
Dividends paid	(1,386)	
Net cash used in financing activities		**(841)**
Net decrease in cash and cash equivalents		**(43)**
Cash and cash equivalents at the start of the year		107
Cash and cash equivalents at the end of the year		64

W1 Profit from operations

	£000
Decrease in retained earnings:	
Retained earnings at 31 December 20-8	4,162
Less Retained earnings at 31 December 20-7	4,275
	(113)
Add back:	
Dividends paid	1,386
Tax provision	380
Finance costs	152
Profit from operations	1,805

W2 Cost of non-current assets sold

	£000
Cost at 31 December 20-8	8,570
Less Additions	784
	7,786
Less Cost at 31 December 20-7	7,825
Cost of non-current assets sold	(39)

W3 Profit on disposal of non-current assets

	£000
Cost of non-current assets sold (W2)	39
Less Depreciation	(28)
	11
Less Sale proceeds	(14)
Profit on disposal	(3)

W4 Receipts from issue of share capital

	£000
Increase in share capital:	
Ordinary shares at 31 December 20-8	1,700
Share premium at 31 December 20-8	280
	1,980
Less	
Ordinary shares at 31 December 20-7	1,500
Share premium at 31 December 20-7	250
	1,750
Issue of share capital	230

CHAPTER 8: INTERPRETATION OF ACCOUNTING INFORMATION

1. A

    Dividend yield = dividend per share ÷ market price per share × 100

    Dividend per share = £360,000 ÷ 300,000 = £1.20

    Dividend yield = £1.20 ÷ £4.80 × 100 = 25%

2. B

    Earnings per share = profit after tax ÷ number of issued shares

    = £450,000 ÷ 300,000 = £1.50

3. A

    Dividend cover = profit after tax ÷ ordinary share dividends paid

    = £450,000 ÷ £360,000 = 1.25 times

4. B

    Price earnings = current market price per share ÷ earnings per share

    = £4.80 ÷ £1.50 (see answer 2) = 3.20

5. D

    Interest cover = profit before interest and tax ÷ interest payable

    = £630,000 ÷ £20,000 = 31.50 times

6. (c)

7. Limitations of financial ratios to make an investment decision include:

- the calculations are based on information which is historic, they do not reflect what the state of the companies are at present or in the future.

- the financial statements of the two companies may have been prepared using different accounting policies, such as the depreciation policy, this may make comparisons difficult.

- the impact of inflation is not usually taken into account in the preparation of financial statements and most items are recorded at their original cost, so this could distort comparisons.

- a 'poor' ratio does not necessarily mean poor performance, a company may have been operating successfully with similar ratios for a long time, therefore ratios should be considered alongside other available information.

8.

Ratio	30 April 20-8	Workings
Gross profit margin	26%	£2,808,000 ÷ £10,800,000 × 100 = 26%
Profit in relation to revenue	12%	£1,296,000 ÷ £10,800,000 × 100 = 12%
Return on capital employed	80.15%	£1,486,000 ÷ (£1,356,000 + £498,000) × 100 = 80.15%
Interest cover	7.82 times	£1,486,000 ÷ £190,000 = 7.82 times
Current ratio	1.30 : 1	£3,504,000 ÷ £2,700,000 = 1.30 : 1
Liquid capital ratio	1.06 : 1	(£3,504,000 - £654,000) ÷ £2,700,000 = 1.06 : 1
Trade receivables days	96.32 days	£2,850,000 ÷ £10,800,000 × 365 = 96.32 days
Trade payable days	79.90 days	£1,750,000 ÷ £7,994,000 × 365 = 79.90 days
Rate of inventory turnover days	29.82 days	(£652,000 + £654,000) ÷ 2 ÷ £7,992,000 × 365 = 29.82 days
Capital gearing	26.86%	£498,000 ÷ (£498,000 + £1,356,000) × 100 = 26.86%

9.

REPORT
To: Mike
From: AQA accounting student
Subject: Potential investment in Calvin Ltd
Date: Today

I have reviewed the financial statements and ratios for Calvin Ltd and identified the following:

Profitability

The gross profit and profit from operations have both increased, however, there has been a decline in both the gross profit margin (35% to 26%) and the profit in relation to revenue (19% to 12%).

The decrease in gross profit margin is probably due to a decrease in selling price, as sales have almost doubled, and this would suggest a greater volume of sales than in the previous year, it could indicate that the company is growing too rapidly, which could be worrying. However, overhead control would appear to be good as the percentage fall in the profit relation to revenue is lower than the fall in the gross profit margin.

The return on capital employed has more than doubled which is a good sign, however, it is largely due to the decrease in the capital employed.

The finance costs have increased vastly, and interest cover has fallen from over 60 times, to just below eight times. The increased finance costs appear to have been due to the use of a bank overdraft as opposed to a long-term loan in the previous year, which indicates the company is riskier than it was previously.

Liquidity

Both the current and liquid capital ratios have fallen, which is a cause for concern.

Although inventory has remained constant, there has been a big increase in both trade receivables and trade payables, and the company has moved from money in the bank to a large overdraft.

Efficiency

Trade receivables days have increased by approximately 34 days, which means customers are taking longer to pay. This may be due to offering customers extended credit periods to encourage them to buy more.

Trade payable days have also increased by around 40 days, this indicates that the company is struggling to pay its debts on time, which could be due to customers taking longer to pay.

The rate of inventory turnover has fallen by approximately 20 days, this could mean that the company is struggling to pay for inventory, or the increase in sales has meant that it is being used more quickly than previously. If inventory levels become too low, there may be insufficient levels to meet future demand.

Capital structure

A comparison of the gearing shows that there has been a slight improvement from 28.33% to 26.86%, this means that less reliance is placed on the banks for long-term funding.

However, the increase in the bank overdraft and finance costs may indicate that banks are no longer willing to lend the company money, this makes the company much riskier.

Conclusion

I do not recommend that you invest in Calvin Ltd at this point in time, it may be worth seeking some further information from the company about its current financial position.

Note: In a question of this nature, make sure you are able to back up your decision with valid points.

10.

Differences between the profit from operations and the fall in the bank balance are due to:

- profit from operations is the surplus of income over expenditure for the financial period and adjustments are made for accruals, prepayments and non-cash items (such as depreciation)

- the bank balance is what the company physically has in cash at the end of the year, in this case it is overdrawn and therefore owes money to the bank.

The statement of cash flows shows the cash which has gone in and out of the company in the last year; explanations of the figures for Turkish Baths plc are:

Cash from operating activities

In this section depreciation of £516,000 has been added back to profit, as it is a non-cash item.

Inventory has increased by £502,000, which suggests that the company has bought more, and cash has decreased.

Trade receivables have also increased by £368,000. This would indicate that revenue is higher, or credit control processes are not working effectively, and cash has decreased.

There is an increase in trade payables, but the amount is not as significant as the increase in inventory. This increases the cash by £31,000.

Net cash from operating activities

The profit from operations does not reflect the interest and tax payments which have been paid out of the bank, totalling £771,000.

Investing activities

The purchase of non-current assets is not reflected in the profit from operations and cash has decreased by £2,584,000 from investing in them.

Financing activities

There has been a decrease in the non-current loan of £580,000, which is not included in profit from operations.

Dividends paid to shareholders total £334,000. These are not included in profit from operations.

Both figures reduce the amount of cash.

CHAPTER 9: ACCOUNTING REGULATIONS AND ETHICS

1. (a), (b) and (d) are true.

(c) is false.

2. B

3. C

4. B

5. C

6. Safeguards include any three from:

- corporate governance regulations
- education and training requirements from professional bodies
- continuing professional development
- relevant experience
- external review of work
- professional and regulatory monitoring
- adherence to professional standards
- disciplinary procedures
- policies and procedures to ensure compliance.

    Note: The list is not exhaustive and other points may be valid.

7. Corporate Social Responsibility policies include any two from:

    - using local or ethical suppliers
    - running fuel efficient vehicles
    - setting recycling targets
    - encouraging employees to carry out voluntary activities for the local community or charities
    - allowing flexible working arrangements for employees.

        Note: The list is not exhaustive and other examples may be valid.

8. An accountant in practice should:

    - establish the facts
    - determine whether the acts are unethical or illegal
    - seek external advice if required, from their professional body or a legal advisor
    - consider ceasing to work for the client
    - if the law has been broken, the accountant may have an obligation to report it to the relevant authority.

        Note: The list is not exhaustive and other steps may be valid.

MANAGEMENT ACCOUNTING
ANSWERS

CHAPTER 10: MANAGEMENT ACCOUNTING: THE USE OF BUDGETS

1. (b), (c) and (d) relate to management accounting.

(a) relates to financial accounting.

2. (c)

3. D

Closing inventory is 1,965 units (7,860 × 25%).

Production budget = 6,240 − 1,560 + 1,965 = 6,645 units.

4. B

	£	
July purchases	10,500	(£21,000 × 50%)
August purchases	11,500	(£23,000 × 50%)
Less August cash discount	(230)	(£11,500 × 2%)
	21,770	

5. 50 hours shortfall

	Hours	
Hours required	1,050	(3.5 × 300)
Hours available	(1,000)	
Shortfall	50	

6.

	Jan	Feb	Mar	Apr
Units	800	880	880	836
	£	£	£	£
Sales (units × £15.50)	12,400	13,640	13,640	12,958

	May	Jun	Total
Units	800	920	5,116
	£	£	£
Sales (units × £15.50)	12,400	14,260	79,298

Workings:

February and March	800 units × 1.1 = 880 units
April	880 units × 0.95 = 836 units
June	800 units × 1.15 = 920 units

7.

	Month 1	Month 2	Month 3	Month 4
Production budget	Units	Units	Units	Units
Sales	500	600	560	650
Opening inventory	(125)	(150)	(140)	(160)
Closing inventory (W1)	150	140	160	150
Production	**525**	**590**	**580**	**640**
Purchases budget	kg	kg	kg	kg
Production (× 3)	1,575	1,770	1,740	1,920
Opening inventory	(315)	(354)	(348)	(384)
Closing inventory (W2)	354	348	384	366
Purchases	**1,614**	**1,764**	**1,776**	**1,902**
Purchases budget	£	£	£	£
Purchases (× £0.50)	**807**	**882**	**888**	**951**

W1 Closing inventory (finished units)

    Month 1   600 × 25% = 150

    Month 2   560 × 25% = 140

    Month 3   650 × 25% = 162.5, but cannot exceed 160

    Month 4   600 × 25% = 150

W2 Closing inventory (materials)

    Month 1   1,770 ÷ 5 = 354

    Month 2   1,740 ÷ 5 = 348

    Month 3   1,920 ÷ 5 = 384

    Month 4   1,830 ÷ 5 = 366

8.

	April	May	June
Receipts:	£	£	£
Month of sale (W1)	12,000	15,000	18,000
Less Discount (W2)	(360)	(450)	(540)
Month after sale (W3)	16,800	18,000	22,500
Less Irrecoverable debts (W4)	(840)	(900)	(1,125)
Total	**27,600**	**31,650**	**38,835**

W1 Month of sale

    April   £30,000 × 40% = £12,000

    May   £37,500 × 40% = £15,000

    June   £45,000 × 40% = £18,000

W2 Discount

    April   £12,000 × 3% = £360

    May   £15,000 × 3% = £450

    June   £18,000 × 3% = £540

W3 Month after sale

    April   £16,800

    May   £30,000 × 60% = £18,000

    June   £37,500 × 60% = £22,500

W4 Irrecoverable debts

    April   £16,800 × 5% = £840

    May   £18,000 × 5% = £900

    June   £22,500 × 5% = £1,125

9.

(a) Cash budget for 'The IT Shop' for the period ended 31 March 20-8:

	January	February	March
	£	£	£
Receipts:			
Cash sales	1,500	1,600	1,650
Credit sales (W1)	18,293	21,284	24,066
Total receipts	**19,793**	**22,884**	**25,716**
Payments:			
Purchases	4,250	5,750	6,000
Shop refit	–	28,000	–
Operating expenses	3,600	3,600	3,600
Drawings	1,800	1,800	1,800
Total payments	**9,650**	**39,150**	**11,400**
Net cash flow	10,143	(16,266)	14,316
Opening bank/(overdraft)	5,866	16,009	(257)
Closing bank/(overdraft)	16,009	(257)	14,059

W1 Credit sales

Month of sale:	Jan (£)	Feb (£)	Mar (£)	Notes
Nov	4,800	–	–	
Dec	6,800	5,100	–	F £11,900 – £6,800
Jan	6,900	9,200	6,900	J £23,000 × 30%
				F £23,000 × 40%
				M £23,000 × 30%
Discount Jan	(207)	–	–	£6,900 × 3%
Feb	–	7,200	9,600	F £24,000 × 30%
				M £24,000 × 40%
Discount Feb	–	(216)	–	£7,200 × 3%
Mar	–	–	7,800	M £26,000 × 30%
Discount Mar	–	–	(234)	£7,800 × 3%
Total	18,293	21,284	24,066	

(b) Increase in overdraft:

- based on the figures in the cash budget the bank will be overdrawn in February only, by £257
- this figure is within the overdraft limit of £1,000
- if sales do not reach the forecast or the shop refit cost is higher than anticipated, it may be advisable to ask for a temporary higher increase in the limit.

10.   'The IT Shop'

Budgeted Income Statement for the period ended 31 March 20-8

	£	£
Revenue (W1)		77,750
Opening inventory	1,684	
Purchases (W2)	18,250	
	19,934	
Less Closing inventory	2,400	
Cost of sales		17,534
Gross profit		60,216
Less Expenses:		
Discounts allowed (W3)	657	
Operating expenses (W4)	10,800	
Depreciation	1,500	
		12,957
Net profit for the period		47,259

W1   Revenue

	£	
Jan	24,500	(£1,500 + £23,000)
Feb	25,600	(£1,600 + £24,000)
Mar	27,650	(£1,650 + £26,000)
	77,750	

W2	Purchases	
		£
	Jan	5,750
	Feb	6,000
	Mar	6,500
		18,250

W3	Discounts allowed	
		£
	Jan	207
	Feb	216
	Mar	234
		657

W4	Operating expenses	
		£
	Jan	3,600
	Feb	3,600
	Mar	3,600
		10,800

'The IT Shop'
Budgeted Statement of Financial Position as at 31 March 20-8

	£	£	£
Non-current assets			
Carrying value (W5)			31,500
Current assets			
Inventory		2,400	
Trade receivables (W6)		25,400	
Bank		14,059	
		41,859	
Less Current liabilities			
Trade payables	6,500		
		6,500	
Net current assets			35,359
NET ASSETS			66,859
FINANCED BY			
Opening capital			25,000
Add Profit for the period			47,259
			72,259
Less Drawings (W7)			5,400
			66,859

W5	Non-current assets		
		£	
	At 1 January 20-8	5,000	
	Shop refit	28,000	
	Less Depreciation	(1,500)	
		31,500	

W6	Trade receivables		
		£	
	Feb	7,200	(£24,000 × 30%)
	Mar	18,200	(£26,000 × 70%)
		25,400	

W7	Drawings		
		£	
	Jan	1,800	
	Feb	1,800	
	Mar	1,800	
		5,400	

CHAPTER 11: ABSORPTION AND ACTIVITY BASED COSTING

1. (c)

2. (a) relates to activity based costing.

(b) and (d) relate to marginal costing.

(c) relates to absorption costing.

3. D

(£450 + £510 + £480) ÷ 150 = £9.60 per unit

4. A

£2.25 + £1.50 = £3.75 per unit

5. D

(£22,000 + £88,000) ÷ (£100 − £45) = 2,000 units

6. C

(£360 + £40) × 1.25 = £500

7.

	Honey Dew	Sunflower
	£	£
Direct materials (W1)	29,600	51,000
Direct labour (W2)	7,200	21,600
Total direct cost	36,800	72,600
Overheads:		
Machinery set-ups (W3)	13,200	52,800
Quality inspections (W4)	2,000	12,000
Total cost	52,000	137,400
Total cost per unit (W5)	**13.00**	**22.90**
Selling price per unit	18.00	22.50
Profit/(loss) per unit	**5.00**	**(0.40)**

W1   Direct materials

  Honey Dew   £7.40 × 4,000 = £29,600

  Sunflower   £8.50 × 6,000 = £51,000

W2   Direct labour

  Honey Dew   £1.80 × 4,000 = £7,200

  Sunflower   £3.60 × 6,000 = £21,600

W3   Machinery set-ups

				£
Honey Dew	4,000 × 3 set-ups	12,000	× £1.10	13,200
Sunflower	6,000 × 8 set-ups	48,000	× £1.10	52,800
Total set-ups		60,000		66,000
Cost per set-up	£66,000 ÷ 60,000	£1.10		

W4 Quality inspections

				£
Honey Dew	4,000 × 1 inspection	4,000	× £0.50	2,000
Sunflower	6,000 × 4 inspections	24,000	× £0.50	12,000
Total inspections		28,000		14,000

Cost per inspection   £14,000 ÷ 28,000   £0.50

W5 Total cost per unit

Honey Dew   £52,000 ÷ 4,000 = £13.00

Sunflower   £137,400 ÷ 6,000 = £22.90

8. Any one benefit and one limitation for each from the following:

	Benefit	Limitation
Marginal costing	Simple to calculate and understand	Not acceptable under IAS 2
Marginal costing	Can assist with make or buy decisions	Cost per unit does not include any overhead, therefore selling price is less accurate
Absorption costing	Acceptable under IAS 2	Not useful for short term decision making
Absorption costing	Cost per unit includes overhead absorbed using labour or machine hours, which is fine for traditional businesses	Less accurate method of establishing selling price where complex overheads are involved
Activity based costing	Acceptable under IAS 2	Time consuming to set-up and record
Activity based costing	Uses activities to absorb overheads, which should make the calculation of the selling price more accurate	Selecting cost drivers can be difficult

CHAPTER 12: OVERHEADS AND OVERHEAD ABSORPTION

1. (b)

2. C

    £500,000 ÷ 10,000 = £50

3. C

    £61,000 ÷ 100 × 52 = £31,720

4. A and D

    Production £80,000 ÷ 4,000 = £20 per hour

    Packing £43,200 ÷ 2,880 = £15 per hour

5. A

    (£28,500 ÷ 1,400,000 × 490,000) + £26,700 = £36,675

6. (a) £1,765 over absorbed

		£
Overhead absorbed	18,375 × £9.20	169,050
Actual overhead		167,285
Over absorbed		1,765

(b) An alternative method is labour hours.

The overhead is absorbed on the basis of the number of direct labour hours worked.

This method would be more appropriate for a department which is very labour intensive and has a high proportion of overhead incurred from labour related activities, rather than machine-based activities.

7. (a) and (b)

Overheads	Basis of apportionment	Total overheads £	Hair £	Beauty £	Admin. £
Supervisor's salary – hair	Allocated	35,665	35,665	–	–
Supervisor's salary – beauty	Allocated	32,135	–	32,135	–
Receptionist's salary (W1)	Use of receptionist's time	17,500	10,500	7,000	–
Administration salaries	Allocated	48,000	–	–	48,000
Rent and rates (W2)	Floor area	50,000	24,000	15,000	11,000
Buildings insurance (W3)	Floor area	15,000	7,200	4,500	3,300
Equipment depreciation (W4)	Carrying amount of equipment	9,000	3,600	4,950	450
Equipment insurance (W5)	Carrying amount of equipment	6,000	2,400	3,300	300
Total overheads (a)		213,300	83,365	66,885	63,050
Re-apportion administration (W6)		–	44,135	18,915	(63,050)
Total overheads (b)		213,300	127,500	85,800	–

(c) Overhead absorption rates:

    Hair   £127,500 ÷ 8,500 = £15.00 per hour

    Beauty   £85,800 ÷ 5,200 = £16.50 per hour

W1   Receptionist's salary

      Hair   £17,500 × 60% = £10,500

      Beauty   £17,500 × 40% = £7,000

W2   Rent and rates

	Square metres		£
Hair	240	240 ÷ 500 × £50,000	24,000
Beauty	150	150 ÷ 500 × £50,000	15,000
Administration	110	110 ÷ 500 × £50,000	11,000
Total floor area	500		50,000

W3   Buildings insurance

	Square metres		£
Hair	240	240 ÷ 500 × £15,000	7,200
Beauty	150	150 ÷ 500 × £15,000	4,500
Administration	110	110 ÷ 500 × £15,000	3,300
Total floor area	500		15,000

W4 Equipment depreciation

	Equipment £		£
Hair	18,000	18,000 ÷ 45,000 × £9,000	3,600
Beauty	24,750	24,750 ÷ 45,000 × £9,000	4,950
Administration	2,250	2,250 ÷ 45,000 × £9,000	450
Total carrying amount	45,000		9,000

W5 Equipment insurance

	Equipment £		£
Hair	18,000	18,000 ÷ 45,000 × £6,000	2,400
Beauty	24,750	24,750 ÷ 45,000 × £6,000	3,300
Administration	2,250	2,250 ÷ 45,000 × £6,000	300
Total carrying amount	45,000		6,000

W6 Re-apportion administration overheads

Hair £63,050 × 70% = £44,135

Beauty £63,050 × 30% = £18,915

CHAPTER 13: STANDARD COSTING AND VARIANCE ANALYSIS

1. D

   (1,400 − 1,200) × £12 = £2,400 Fav

2. A

   £15,200 − (1,400 × £12) = £1,600 Adv

3. B

   1,100 × (£22.00 − £21.50) = £550 Fav

4. C

   £22.00 × (1,000 − 1,100) = £2,200 Adv

5. (a) and (d) are correct.

   (b) and (c) are incorrect.

6. (c)

7. (a) Materials variance

   (580 × £10.50) − (560 × £11.75) = £490 Adv

   Possible causes could be:

   - this is the overall variance, there will probably be some link between the price (£700 Adv) and usage (£210 Fav) variances, such as:
     - a better quality of material has been used, but at a higher price

   (b) Materials price variance

   560 × (£10.50 − £11.75) = £700 Adv

   Possible causes could be:

   - changing to a more expensive supplier
   - not taking advantage of discounts available
   - incorrect standard
   - unexpected inflation

   (c) Materials usage variance

   £10.50 × (580 − 560) = £210 Fav

   Possible causes could be:

   - better quality of material
   - more experienced staff, therefore generating less wastage
   - incorrect standard

8. (a)

	Original budget	Flexed budget	Actual	Variances
	£	£	£	£
Sales (W1)	96,000	108,000 volume 12,000 Fav	103,500	4,500 Adv price 4,500 Adv
Less costs				
Labour (W2)	28,000	31,500	37,440	5,940 Adv rate 3,510 Fav efficiency 9,450 Adv
Contribution	68,000	76,500	66,060	10,440 Adv
Overheads	30,000	30,000	30,000	–
Profit	38,000	46,500	36,060	10,440 Adv

W1 Sales

Original budget 80 × £1,200 = £96,000

Flexed budget 90 × £1,200 = £108,000

Actual 90 × £1,150 = £103,500

W2 Labour

Original budget 10 × 80 × £35 = £28,000

Flexed budget 10 × 90 × £35 = £31,500

Actual 13 × 90 × £32 = £37,440

(b) The actual sales price is lower than budget, which could be due to:

- wanting to secure more projects
- competition in the market place
- discounts for repeat business

The volume of sales is higher than the budget; causes could be:

- lower sales prices
- less competition
- seasonal increases

The labour rate is lower than allowed for, possibly due to:

- lower grade of labour used
- reductions in the level of wage rates

The labour efficiency is lower than expected, this could be due to:

- lower grade of labour used
- projects could be more complex than anticipated

CHAPTER 14: CAPITAL INVESTMENT APPRAISAL

1. C

Year	Net cash flow	Cumulative net cash flow
	£	£
0	(700,000)	(700,000)
1	(100,000)	(800,000)
2	600,000	(200,000)
3	850,000	650,000
4	250,000	900,000

Payback = 2 years + (200,000/850,000 × 365) = 2 years and 86 days

2. A

Year	Net cash flow	Discount factor	Discounted cash flow
	£	£	£
0	(700,000)	1.0	(700,000)
1	(100,000)	0.909	(90,900)
2	600,000	0.826	495,600
3	850,000	0.751	638,350
4	250,000	0.683	170,750
Net present value			513,800

3. (c)

4. **Benefits** of the payback method include any one from the following:

- Payback is easy to calculate, cash inflows and outflows are added together cumulatively for each year, to identify when the initial cost of investment is repaid.

- Payback is easy to understand, by calculating the cumulative cash flows, it can be seen when an investment will be repaid.

- With payback, emphasis is placed on the earliest cash flows, which are probably more accurate than cash flows from a long time in the future.

Limitations of the payback method include any one from the following:

- Cash flow estimates may be inaccurate, which could mean that the wrong project is selected.

- Payback does not consider the cash flows after the payback period, which may have a major impact on a project.

- Payback does not take into account the time value of money, it assumes that a pound received now will be worth the same as a pound received in the future.

5. **Financial** factors include any two from the following:

- initial capital requirements
- working capital requirements
- costs of borrowing
- taxation
- accuracy of cash flow and budget forecasts

Non-financial factors include any two from the following:

- expertise of employees required
- recruitment and training needs
- impact on the local economy and environment
- availability of material requirements

answers – Chapter 14

6. (a)

Year	Net cash flow	Cumulative net cash flow
	£	£
0	(88,000)	(88,000)
1	23,000	(65,000)
2	65,000	–
3	72,000	72,000
4	87,000	159,000
5	12,000	171,000

Payback = 2 years

Net cash flow workings

Year 1 £76,000 – £38,000 – £15,000 = £23,000

Year 2 £160,000 – £80,000 – £15,000 = £65,000

Year 3 £174,000 – £87,000 – £15,000 = £72,000

Year 4 £204,000 – £102,000 – £15,000 = £87,000

Year 5 £54,000 – £27,000 – £15,000 = £12,000

(b)

Year	Net cash flow	Discount factor	Discounted cash flow
	£	£	£
0	(88,000)	1.0	(88,000)
1	23,000	0.909	20,907
2	65,000	0.826	53,690
3	72,000	0.751	54,072
4	87,000	0.683	59,421
5	12,000	0.621	7,452
Net present value			107,542

7. Assessment of the financial implications of the two projects:

   Initial investment – X is preferable:

   - the amount for Y is double that of X
   - the initial investment must be financed by a loan
   - the interest rate on the loan is variable, therefore it could increase

   Net present value – Y is preferable:

   - the net present value of Y is much higher than X, meaning it will generate more cash
   - a change in the interest rate would change the net present values of the projects
   - a change in the return on capital employed would also change the net present values of the projects
   - how reliable are the cash flow forecasts?

   Payback period – Y is preferable:

   - Y pays back in two years, whereas X takes three years
   - however, the cash flows after the payback period are not taken into account
   - how reliable are the cash flow forecasts?

   Estimated life of the project – X is preferable:

   - the project life of X is three years more than Y
   - how reliable are the estimates?
   - what happens at the end of the project, can the life be extended?

Assessment of the non-financial implications of the two projects:

Project X

- local residents are likely to object to the closure of a thriving community meeting place
- local jobs will not be created
- a new shop could cause disruption to local roads and parking

Project Y

- local jobs will be created in a deprived area
- sports facilities will become all-inclusive
- there are health benefits to encourage sports for all the local community
- there may be disruption to local roads and parking

Conclusion

Based on the financial factors, project X is less risky as the investment is lower, however, based on long-term cash flows and the assumption that the overall aim is to maximise the net present value, the choice should be project Y.

The non-financial factors would also indicate that the choice should be project Y.

However, Nottingsham Sports Ltd could also consider helping the community shop in project X to become more profitable by offering a range of sportswear in the existing shop.

Note: In a question of this nature, make sure you are able to back up your decision with valid points.